Forgotten Corners:

Essays in Search of an Island's Soul

Copyright: Pete Hay 2019

This book is copyright. Apart from any fair dealing for the purposes of study and research, criticism, review, or as otherwise permitted under the Copyright Act, no part may be reproduced in any manner without first gaining written permission from the author.

Walleah Press
PO Box 368
North Hobart
Tasmania 7002 Australia
ralph.wessman@walleahpress.com.au

Cover image: Matthew Newton
(King's Run, near Arthur River, Tasmania)

ISBN: 978-1-877010-92-7

Forgotten Corners:

Essays in Search of an Island's Soul

Pete Hay

Table of Contents

Preface	1
The Vast Grey Wall	3
What I Did on My Holidays	7
Not Far From Here – Thoughts on the Cataclysmic Art of Richard Wastell	22
From a Suitcase in Maritime Canada	26
Defending the Wild Lands	42
'They Might As Well Cut My Brain Out'	56
Going on 'The River'	67
A Democrat's Lament	72
Flow and Stasis on Tasmania's West Coast – The Emplaced Art of Raymond Arnold	82
Politics and Primordial Time – Neil Hoffman's Grand and Seamless Aesthetic	86
The Gallopers – 'Time Gone By Is Here Today'	94
Ghosts in the Jungle	99
Murphy versus Descartes – *Domum Invenio, Ergo Sum*	112
Painting the Shape of the Wind – Pattern and Chaos in the Island Art of Sue Lovegrove	120
'The Pulp' – Reflections on an Island Dreaming	124
To Tilt at Windmills, and So Change the World	127
Art in the Forgotten Corners – The Photojournalism of Matthew Newton	132
The Breath of Vast Time	136
On Skullbone Plains – Considering the False Contestation of Culture and Nature	144
On Albatross Island – Science and Myth	149

Resurrecting the Public Interest – On Logging   157
   Lapoinya
Schismatic Tasmania and the Politics of Writing   161
Books Are the New Zucchini   168

Preface

It's 18 years since Walleah Press published *Vandiemonian Essays*, since when the times have changed – and the publishing landscape even more dramatically. Twixt then and now the digital revolution has arrived, and publication options for the essay writer have snowballed. Under such circumstances, can a case be made for a retrospective collection? On paper, between hard covers? As opposed to a modest, undemonstrative scarcely-regarded posting on the web? Here today, digital dross tomorrow?

It may be so. It may be that an old-fashioned collection of essays in book form is an authorial indulgence, and to be resisted. The trouble with this is that I'm old school, and I can't change. A dinosaur with, at best, only a few short years of literary output remaining. So I hope you'll cut me some slack. Here, then, is my old-medium collection. A sort of next generation *Vandiemonian Essays*, thought by its author a fit companion to rub alongside that earlier volume on a bookshelf.

Is there a theme that connects these essays? Well, yes – they all, separately and collectively, seek to shed light on a certain grain within Tasmanian life, the various creative and dissident currents that even now bear the tenacious Vandiemonian spirit. 'Dissident'? Indeed so – as James Boyce so brilliantly demonstrated in his modern classic, *Van Diemen's Land,* there is a stubborn current of resistance to the political economy imposed upon us by those who wield power (those people and institutions with little understanding of our island's vernacular ecologies and communal folkways). It amounts to a cleavage between those who see the island as raw material awaiting the uncaring inscription of capital – without value until such inscriptions have been made – and those whose ways of acting within and understanding the island are driven by a pure, intrinsic love, and are, hence, unavoidably oppositional.

In one of the essays contained within these pages, this is argued explicitly. But even when such is not the case, even when there is no apparent cultural/political 'point' to a particular essay, that resistant spirit remains the thread that binds these pieces into a themed collection. The people of whom I have written are those who bear, sometimes without any great awareness of same, a counteractive mode of being Tasmanian. This can be overtly so. Or it can simply be found within the sum of who they are, of what they say, of what they do.

Which brings me to the other reason why I have gathered this collection together. I'm starting to feel lonely. And wanting to lay down a manifesto. I hope I'm wrong, but I have a sense that the Vandiemonian trope no longer energises island creatives to the extent that it did not very many years ago. And if that is so, to my mind therein lies tragedy.

Anyway, 18 years' worth of a poet's essays follow. And I hope you enjoy them.

Pete

The Vast Grey Wall

(Originally published in *Reflections on Social Justice: Reclaiming Our Identity as a Nation with a Heart and a Soul*, Anglicare Social Action and Research Centre, 2003. The Prime Minister at the time was, of course, John Howard. It is quite a while since this essay was written, but reading it now, it seems to me that the times have passed it by only in small part.)

I am at the launch of *Whitewash,* Robert Manne's edited riposte to Keith Windschuttle's *(F)fabrication*. A moment ago it was my privilege to introduce Greg Lehman to a standing-room only audience. I called him my very great friend and a great Aboriginal Tasmanian. Greg speaks, and he summons words from a deep, primal hurt.

A certain view of his people has been propagated by Windschuttle and enthusiastically endorsed by a raft of the country's cultural arbiters, not least among whom is the Prime Minister himself. This *certain* view portrays the people who were here when we arrived smug, uninvited and assured of our cultural superiority as degenerate, treacherous, ignoble, debased, callously evil. Which is to say, the very antithesis of *us*. Windschuttle's *Fabrication* is possibly the meanest book ever published in Australia. It is ill-disguised racial primitivism – ideology pretending to be scholarship. Were it a single idiosyncratic voice, one soundly condemned by decent, justice-informed shapers and interpreters of Australian culture, it would scarcely have mattered. It is the enthusiasm – the *passion*, the utter *glee* – with which its ideological construct of pre-encounter Aboriginality was welcomed by those holding cultural and political power that is the appalling thing.

Thus it must seem to Greg Lehman. I can only imagine the knife-edge of his hurt. He wrenches words to the surface, and his pain is utterly raw. This speech might just be the hardest thing he has ever had to do in his life. Now, spent and overcome, he sits through the rest of the evening with his face buried in his hands. He is beyond the reach of conventional offerings of comfort.

*

Writing of my book, *Vandiemonian Essays*, Martin Flanagan proffered a couple of small and respectful criticisms, one of which is that, within my writing, there is no engagement with questions of Aboriginality. That is true, and there are three reasons for this. The first of these has to do with how it now is for Tasmania's Aboriginal people. I hold a dissident view on a single but key component of the contemporary construction of Aboriginality, and as I do not want to offend those whom I esteem among the Aboriginal people, I prefer to keep this view to myself (though I can assure you that it is not a point of dissent such as to position me anywhere near the camp of the Fabricators!). The second stems from a respect for (though not necessarily agreement with) a prominent view within the Aboriginal community that matters to do with Aboriginal history, culture and identity are 'owned' by Aboriginal people and that we whiteys are re-enacting colonial expropriation when we assume an academic's or a writer's right to probe into such questions. And the third has to do with the *opacity* of the relevant history — and of this source of my reluctance when it comes to Aboriginality I am willing to write.

Despite the fine and dedicated work of the scholars of encounter — those scholars now so unfairly reviled — much of the detail of life before the invasion, and much of the detail of encounter, is not mine for the knowing. 'The time before', I have written in a poem, 'is a vast grey wall'. A porous wall, certainly, but through it I can see only vagaries, not detail. Mere 'shadow-shapes'.

My forebears were early pioneers of the North-West coastal town of Wynyard. The local Aboriginal people were the *Tommeginer*.

By the time the first European settler arrived in Wynyard the Aboriginal people were gone. I have examined the historical record for knowledge of the Tommeginer, and I have learnt that they were 'a warlike people'. I know, too, that the last eight Tommeginer, in 'a sickly state', were among the last of the people to be 'repatriated' by George Augustus Robinson – at the very end of 1834. But I do not know how life was for them in the Table Cape country, and I do not know the events that reduced a mettlesome folk to an ailing band of eight.

On the coast at Fossil Bluff there is an old stone fishtrap. I grew up with the legend that it was of Aboriginal provenance – but, we are told, the Aboriginal people ate no scalefish. What am I to make of the mystery of the fishtrap? It is maddening, because it is a mystery that should be amenable to resolution. Over the years it has acquired, for me, an almost obsessive status. I want to know about the *Tommeginer,* and I want to know why they are gone. Science might, if it eventually chooses, solve the riddle of the fishtrap. That is the most I can hope for. The rest is irretrievable.

*

No details. But there is a sense in which an infatuation with detail is the essence of the problem. To know whether the *Tommeginer* were all but exterminated in this or that unrecorded 'incident', or whether, on such and such a date, x number died or only y, or even whether introduced disease carries the sole or greater culpability, is ultimately of secondary importance to the sheer fact that they are gone, and that they are gone as a direct consequence of our arrival. The Windschuttle case allies a 'scholarship' of nitpickery to a mean-spirited ideology of racially-sourced contempt. Thankfully, James Boyce has brilliantly demonstrated that Windschuttle's scholarship is shoddier by very many degrees than those with whom he takes issue. But we are dealing, I think, with issues that are not, finally, to do with the details of scholarship at all. *The* Tommeginer *are gone and they are gone as a direct consequence of our arrival.*

With that insight I can begin to see the nature and magnitude of the debt owed. I will never know what the people who lived here said or felt about the country that became my boyhood range, how they interacted with each other and with the systems of nature, or how they looked out upon the cosmos. But I know that the people before us lived with and not against the life-sustaining systems of the island – and that this demands respect and acknowledgement, not false and insulting constructs of degeneracy and debasement. The crusaders of the history wars have done enormous damage to the cause of reconciliation. But it is my hope that the damage will not, ultimately, prove irreparable. It is my hope that the realisation will prevail that this *is*, contra Windschuttle, ultimately a moral and not an empirical question, that it is not a matter of dates and footnotes – and that such a realisation will eventually put paid to the false terms of the current 'debate'.

*

Greg Lehman sits with his face in his hands. I am in the presence of an awful desolation, and tonight I am powerless to reach past it. But tomorrow we will sit at someone's kitchen table, we will share food and drink, and conversation will resume. Throughout the country similar encounters will take place. And the great cultural project of our times will again resume its inchingly slow and difficult progress.

What I Did on My Holidays

(Published in *Famous Reporter*, 28, 2004.)

For two consecutive Christmas breaks my schoolboy son tramped the town looking for casual work. Nothing. Not a sniff.

How work has changed since I sallied bravely forth, not all that many years ago, in search of my own first paid employment. How ironic, I thought, as my dispirited son returned from a fruitless beat along Sandy Bay Road, that in a time when casualisation is the name of the game there was no casual work to be had. At a time when workplace flexibility is all the rhetorical rage, no business house in Hobart had the flexibility to find a job for a bright and eager boy on his holidays.

What have we lost? Well, we have lost, or are losing, some things that are not to be lamented. Repetitive, single-process, spirit-crushing assembly lines. The dark and dreary work of remnant nineteenth century industrialism, work demanding such desperate fortitude that it bred a perverse pride in the capacity to 'stick' what most would find too tough, or, worse, too mindless to be endured. It bred a pathological adherence to dirty, destructive work as the work that a 'real' man does. Oh yes, it is not to be lamented that those days have passed. Or are passing – we get a dying echo of this culture in the occasional letter-to-the-editor sneering at limp-wristed greenies who 'would turn real men into basket weavers'.

It is a cheap and facile shot. And what is wrong with basket weaving anyway? It is surely to be preferred to my first job.

*

My home town's most visible contribution to the 1939-45 war effort – apart from its boys – was the flax mill. When I was a boy it was a sad, derelict site on the edge of a doomed and wonderful swamp, and at some unknown adolescent moment I became aware that the last trace of the mill, like the swamp, was gone.

Near here, perhaps on the very spot, a Scotsman new to town set up a brickyard. Enter the world of Blake's dark, satanic mills. No union's civilising presence here; no security of either work or limb. The contract filled, we all got the shove. No notice – it was 'dinna coom in t'moora. Here's y'peey. Coont it afoor y'gae.' Come the next contract we might or might not get a call of 'cn y'steert t'moora?' I did not.

Ah, the brickyard – long gone. It lasted less time and it certainly made less of an imprint upon the town's soul than the flax mill.

There are three jobs in the brickyard, not counting the envied 'plum' that was the defended monopoly of my old schoolmate, Kerry. A prince among peasants, Kerry drives the forklift. Under a hot tin roof sit the two satanic machines. This is literally true: they would absolutely have to be relics from the industrial revolution's brute past. High on top of the machine stands a large box full of dense, dry, clay-ish earth that is destined for brickhood. Perhaps it *is* clay. I stand half in the box, half out, my outer foot wedged against a narrow iron tube, shovelling this infernal, spade-resistant stuff out of the box and into the maw of the machine. Only that round and narrow tube stands between my foot and, three inches away, the enormous cogwheel that mixes the dry stuff with water to produce a wet brick. Of course, though, in these enlightened times there is a protective mechanism to cover the cogwheel. Oh no there is not. But there is no time to worry about this. The machine – a curse upon it – dictates a cracking, a *back*-cracking, pace, and if my flying shovel can't keep up with it the bricks come out crumbly, half-formed and useless, and there is a detestable Scottish person threatening physical violence, and wondering aloud whether, if he sacks me on the spot, he can get someone in within the hour to replace me.

That is the good job.

Down on the ground a conveyor belt brings forth a steady stream of wet bricks. These are to be taken from the belt and stacked on a palette for drying. They have to be placed in a certain complex way so that the drying is thorough and even. Bloody hell! I've stuffed it – now I have to pull the stack apart and rebuild it, contending the while with the uncaring machine's unslowed output. A curse upon the machine. Back to 'normal' and I work doubled over. Take brick from belt, swivel, put brick on palette, swivel, take brick from belt, swivel… Luxury is a moment snatched upright. There is little time for talk, except to say, as we two palette-stackers do, every five minutes, 'me back aches t'buggery'. That's not the worst of it. Here's the worst of it. Before stacking, the brick has to be cleaned off – just a sweep of the hand to rid it of extraneous matter. But – the bricks have slivers of compressed stone embedded in them. They are razor-edged and they cut your hands to bloody strips. The caring, generous boss gives us gloves – but you need too much handling precision in this job and the gloves are useless. Pretty soon I am too. Employer intervention pends. After two days I will be sent back to the maw and the cogwheel so my hands can recover in the blistering grip of a shovel – oh, saintly paragon of capitalist compassion! But that is ahead of me. The palette grows. Comes Kerry with the forking truck to take it away, replace it with an empty – and I swap to the empty palette already there on the other side of the conveyor so there is no break in production. Kerry hurtles around with a huge grin on his face. He's having a great time. A curse upon him, too.

We don't know it, but the boss's contractual obligations loom. The furnace roars. The yard fills with bricks. Comes a day the cursed and satanic and machines remain idle, and we are sent to load the trucks. Out in the sun, you beauty! I grab my hat. I climb onto the tray of the first truck. Farewell to the hat, sailing away on the furnace draft, the furnace as rapacious as the boss, my good old hat flying straight down the flue. But now I am looking up at a mountain of bricks, and up there sits Lofty. Lofty is a legend. He works like a threshing machine. He is every bit as tall as his name suggests, a long streak of knucklebone and gristle, with a great crescent hooter in the middle of his face, lank hair, large expressive eyes, and today there is a signifying grin on his dial. 'Put yr gloves on boy', he says, 'I kin promise you yr gunna need them.'

I put the gloves on. Down comes a brick. I catch it. Piece of cake. Another brick. Easy. But now Lofty looks down and he says, 'we'll have to speed her up. Kin y'manage two?' Give it a go. Sweating beside me on the truck, Jonah gasps out a word from the wise. 'Grab the outside bricks and jam the others between them', he says. 'And make sure you get'em, else they'll go straight through and land on yr foot.' Well, okay. Thanks mate. But we're only talking two bricks. Oh no we're not. Lofty's grin is now as satanic as the bloody machines, and just in time I see three bricks come sailing out of the vault of heaven. But I can do three! And now I know what I'm in for, that this is one of those break-the-kid-or-find-his-limit tests of masculine inclusivity, and I knuckle down to it. No-one speaks. I'm small-boned and skinny, but three is easy. Now four. I can do four. Five. I do it, but I know I'm at my limit. The muscles in my shoulders scream as I smack the outer bricks onto the three inners. If I pinch the skin of my hands through the gloves, and I do often, that hurts even more. Here comes six. I do it! But the next time I miss, and I twinkle my toes just in time to avoid the consequences. And suddenly it is back to four, and there it stays for the rest of the day. I can't say they carry me triumphantly around the yard on their shoulders, but they don't lock me out of the tea-room either. I'm feeling pretty good. I'm getting the hang of this job, I think. Then I get the sack.

*

Perhaps I was saved from myself. Perhaps I was about to become a card carrying member of that perverse and macho 'dirty work' elite, and who knows where my life would have gone if I had? But I did not, and now the grim first-wave industrialism of the brickyard is no more. Its passing is not lamented by me, nor, I think, should any of us regret its demise.

There is some good to be taken from this, though. I have seen the worst side of machismo, but it has become apparent, too, that maleness is a more complex construct than can be contained within a stereotype. And even then I knew that this was a dinosaur of a worksite, a throwback to the ragged industrialism of the nineteenth century. It seemed to me that the triumph of the humanistic virtues generally and the civilising hand of unionism in particular meant that such places of employment, rare then, were destined to pass into history (at least in the West — let's proceed in this discussion as if there is no rest of the world).

Ah, progress! Ah, the complacency with which we trust to the vector of history. It is the great modernist myth — the notion that history is an inevitable progression from a given state (today) to a superior state (tomorrow). It is the cornerstone myth of western civilisation. To not believe in progress is to be romantic, or nostalgic, both of which descriptors positively drip with connotations of wrong-headedness.

But the confident assumption of a progressive vector of history is a myth, and our unreflective assumption of its rightness is a structural flaw that greatly undermines our capacity to flexibly respond to technologically-freighted problems. 'You can't stop progress' a big slug of a man, a rural municipal leader, would regularly intone at meetings of a government advisory body that it was my misfortune to chair. It was intended to be a discussion clincher; having so pronounced, he would fold his tree-trunk forearms across his massive chest, and survey the room in aggressive triumph. After a time it became apparent that by 'progress' he merely meant 'economic activity': any form or scale or focus of economic 'development' (another loaded term that carries its ideology within its name) constitutes, in this simple calculus, 'progress'. I recall an interview with a junior American officer in occupied Iraq. His mission is to bring 'progress' to the benighted Iraqis. Questioned about the rich legacy of cultural and artistic achievement of the Iraqi people he is all monosyllabic bewilderment. But then he gets a chance to enthuse over his vision of a McDonalds in every town square and a Wall-Mart on the skirts of every village, and it all becomes plain. Ah, progress.

Of course, this is a tragically misguided, if ideologically potent, notion of 'progress', and one in whose name all manner of violence is committed against the integrity of places and people. 'Progress' does not mean 'economic activity'. It does mean a movement from a given state of affairs to one better. Some economic activity satisfies this definition — and some does not. Whether a proposed development constitutes 'progress' has to be determined anew on a case by case basis, and (it will come as a surprise to government to hear this) when it fails the test, any planned economic activity should not be allowed to proceed.

The brickyard constituted economic activity, but it nowise satisfied the criteria of 'progress'. And as for that inevitably progressive vector of history — well, yes, the disappearance of the brickyard and other workplaces that were characterised by early industrial brutalism — and that were conducive to the very worst constructions of masculinity — is not to be regretted. But is 'progress' really a simple linear incline? It is not — it is something to be secured by people in political combination, often against the odds. Right now the ideas and arguments and hard-won rights that had consigned to history workplaces like the brickyards are under sustained attack. The new institutions of global quasi-government — the World Trade Organisation, the World Bank, the International Monetary Fund — have already successfully promoted a 'right' to the unfettered movement of goods and capital around the globe against the precedence claims of environmental, health and welfare protection. Theirs is a crusade; they are quite unencumbered by doubt. And they have government-backed workplace conditions in the gun.

These days my home town has no dark satanic mill. But it is far from apparent that within a couple of decades it will not again.

Summer on the North-West Coast changed shape when history caught up with the pea-viners. And when it caught up with the 'straddle trucks' – big hollow things like mobile entrance arches, drivers perched way up in the sky, and whether there was a load of sawn timber between their legs or not, they would tear along the road like demented, self-assembled mechano sets. But I only knew these contraptions as mad, exhilarating traffic, so I'll stay with the peas. Which made their own distinctive contribution to those deadly summer roads – not only the flat-trays, peas spilling over open sides like long, lank hair from a bolting death-cart, but also the shapeless, mounding bulk of the mobile viners. Again, though, these latter were mere items within traffic to me – my experience 'on the peas' was confined to intermittent stints in the paddocks and the briefest of spells in the viner just beyond the town's western boundary.

I might have been, for one day, a six-brick catcher at the brickyard, but I'm still a kid with no confidence or muscle-tone. I am given the task that takes the least amount of explaining – keeping the space clear behind the steep, stuttering conveyor belts. Should be easy. Isn't. The fun bits are the real stick-yr-card-in-th-slot timeclock, just like in the movies (though back then I'd have said 'pictures'), and the exotic thrill of night-shift; working in the semi-open of a warm summer night. The vining process is also what we might characterise as industrial-primitive. The machinery is old, simple and cumbersome, all of it housed in an unfloored, galvanised space, and it sets up a fearful clatter. It may be that there is memorable repartee on the belts, but I wouldn't know – the space in which I work is in behind the action, and I have it all to myself. It is like being a one-person backstage crew at the theatre.

And so it is that no-one knows that the flying peastraw dust has me in its grip. I stream from every facial orifice, coughing, sneezing, struggling to find some sustaining oxygen amid the summer's thick and flying strew. I count down every minute to clock-off. The year is just two hours old when I punch my card for the last time, and through my misery I learn that half an hour earlier, 100 yards (it then was) closer to town, the island had chalked up its first road casualty for the new year. A bloke fatally charged for New Year's Eve, foot flat to the floor, roars out of town and into cold clay. Tomorrow I discover that the young man who so randomly cancelled his future was the half-back whose full-blooded attack on the ball set up soft possessions for a country team's young and skinny wingman – me. Back home mum takes one look at my bloated face and decrees this not the holiday job for me.

But over the next few years, when things are desperate, I am sometimes called on to make up a crew out on the trucks. I am inevitably visited by the selfsame affliction, but on the trucks I can manage it better. Here, for the first time, I encounter the politics of the shop floor. Well, it's a long stretch to call the pea paddocks of the North-West Coast a shop floor, but let the metaphor stand. I learn here – and I vividly learn – the venerable industrial ploy of divide and rule. On the trucks there is a driver, who is not part of the crew. The crew consists of the men on the truck's back, forking the peas up the tray to the cabin, working back down the tray until it is loaded. The mechanism that hauls ropes of peas from the ground and deposits them on the tray – it has a name, but I've forgotten it – works to the pace of the truck. The faster the truck moves the faster the peas flop onto the tray and the harder the crews have to work. The crew is paid by the hour. The driver is paid by the load. You get the picture.

Most fist fights are initiated by the driver, irate at the apparent refusal of perfectly hale young men to work to the pace that his greed dictates while the truck slips about on turf slicked by dew or recent rain on a slope that precludes any prospect of keeping your feet – because this is no plain, remember; this is the rolling red-earthed hills and gullies of the North-West Coast. But too much 'trouble-making' and you go on a blacklist – well, the driver doesn't – so now, from the safe vantage of the years I can say that the fist fights didn't happen nearly as often as they should have. I have forgotten so many of the stories from these days, and I hope they will come visiting again in my looming dotage. There was one recurring story, apocryphal by now but always in the telling 'as true as I'm standing here', and perhaps in the beginning it was. A member of the truck crew, work finished, spears his long-handled fork into the ground beside the tray. His mate, not seeing the fork, leaps from the truck, legs a-straddle...

Enough of such unpleasantness. I loved this work. I loved its drama and passion, the life-affirming after-shift ache and weariness from hard and risky toil in the wind and the summer sun. I did it only when a crew was short – just a few times – but I would not put one second of it on the market; not one.

I had learned, on the peas, the sociality of working life – and the contrast with my single day alone and backstage at the viners was impressively stark. This was casual employment so there was no union to be found here, either, but it was a small step from the sociality of the pea harvest to an appreciation of the great civilising good that was trade unionism. Unionism institutionalised the dignity of working life. It was the great educational presence in a working person's life; a mechanism to develop and nurture such satisfying qualities of mind as camaraderie, fellow-feeling, and solidarity. And in giving people a stake in the maintenance of a civilised commonality, unionism acted as a bulwark against widespread alienation. Those who seek the final destruction of unionism know not what they do.

I had learned, too, how work practices can be so devised as to structurally embed injustice. But there was resilience in opposition – inventiveness, and courage to resist discriminatory practice. My workmates, I can see now from the vantage of the years, were autonomous human beings, deeply individual, but possessing the skill to take charge of their lives that comes from pride in membership of a group. The ideologues of the trending neo-conservative political correctness have got it wrong – autonomy is not attainable through society-shunning 'rugged' individualism (the old but newly-fashionable Ayn Rand paradigm). Human autonomy comes from the confidence of identity that membership of a group confers. That is why the compulsive privatisation of life that is so powerfully consequential upon technological change is such a dismaying development. As work, recreation and even neighbourhood are individualised, sociality disappears, a public sphere of and for democratic interaction disappears, and we are left deeply dissatisfied, because we are, at base, social animals, and we cannot be denied sociality and remain content.

I bottomed with the brickyard. I bottomed with the viners. But on my third try I struck gold, a job that sustained me through all my uni vacs, and led to an offer of full-time work ('not out here in the shed though, in the office'). I am in the 'shed' of Clements & Marshall, produce merchants, Burnie. There are stacked bags of 'super', slumped and dumb-heavy. Laying pellets. Blood & bone. But it is fruit and vegetable wholesaling rather than steroids and poisons for the soil that is the mainstay here.

Three times a week I go to Devonport in the big semi (never, in those days, a 'rig'), offsiding for Arthur, who drives that International as if it's a racing car and he's Stirling Moss. At the ferry terminal we wait while folk from the big land to the north, come down to give our cutesy little island the once-over, drive their Cortinas, EHs and Minis, their vans and their shaggin wagons, onto terra firma, mild 'which way do we go now?' concern plain upon their faces. Then we hook up to our container and head back to Burnie for three hard hours of unloading into the coolstore. And I go at it hard, lifting down and hoisting up banana crates a good test of sinew and endurance, but all in a day's work for a six-brick catcher from the brickyard.

Between times I sit in the doorless panel of the delivery van within which Casper scoots around with lettuces and onions and cabbages and oranges for the small and earnest retailers of Burnie. Casper's artless converse is of nothing but cars, though he does know the name of every pedestrian in the street. Or I offside for Tiny on his deliveries to the neighbouring town, my own, and one where my own father once ran what I know now to have been, even then, an old-fashioned grocery shop of bins and scoops and scales.

But the great days arrive in January when handsome Tommy takes his holidays – because then I replace him as the 'china plate' of our West Coast man, loud, ribald, larger-than-life Ted Cox, a man deep in the affections of the folk of the wet wilds of the west. Now, two mornings a week, I'm at work in the pre-dawn dark, loading the almost-breathing monster that fills the shed. By late morning we are away, stopping Tullah, Renison Bell, Rosebery, and arriving at Queenstown in the late afternoon. A quick round of the plethora of dying pubs, and the sad cafes with their hardly-worth-it requests for a few onions, lettuces and tomatoes (for the hamburgers) and, perhaps, if it has been a good week, a couple of bananas to adorn the window for a day or two – and then it is off to check in at Thorn's Queenstown Hotel. Here I face humiliation – the young receptionist is keenly disappointment that I am not the anticipated Heart-Throb Tommy – but I am young, and wounded pride vanishes over a mixed-grill tea and a night in the pub. Here is a pivotal time in a young man's life – especially when closing time arrives and the bar is shut to non-guests, leaving us and the commercial travellers in privileged possession. I soak up yarns of the road. You think all that romance of the road is over-blown; the vacant stuff of myth? I can tell you that you are wrong. In the bar of Thorn's Hotel I grow up fast – and I wish I could report otherwise than that it, along with most of the Queenie pubs, has long since closed its doors.

We are much-valued people in Queenstown. In the denuded gravels of that nationally infamous lunarscape no vegies grow, no fresh fruit. The only fresh food that the hard working folk of the mines get is what we bring in. I have never in my life felt so vital to the scheme of things. In the puff of my pride I take to riding around town shirtless on the prime mover's running board until the local constable quietly suggests to Ted that this really isn't such a good idea.

The day that follows the night in the pub, repeated twice a week for four weeks for three years, is one of the best days of my life. Only the bigger retailers still await our wares – Evans, on the corner (still there), and the mining company's own 'shop', Mount Lyell Stores. Then it's back on the road, but we've all day to get home, and we make a light and a boisterous progress. With one last delivery pending, the nearly-empty Inter barrels into Zeehan, that once-thriving third town of the island, now clinging to life by its toenails. Would it be fair to call it a ghost town? The bored young bucks of Queenstown, needing some action, come to Zeehan in the night to fire the empty houses. Just now these are still in reasonable supply, but you can see there'll be an end to it. I gaze upon the spent glory of the Gaiety, here where Lola Montez never performed, notwithstanding the contrary rumours that have the tenacity of chewing gum in a kid's hair, and I wonder how it would have been to be a raw country miner, testosterone-charged yet perpetually denied, in Lola's merely rumoured audience. Now the Gaiety looks like Lola might if she had spent her last days as an exhausted and impoverished washer-woman – and indeed, there is a string of laundry hanging in the top balcony of the huge old theatre – whilst downstairs that erstwhile lobby of clamour and excitement has been reduced to a row of sorry and flyblown shops. But we are roaring north again, and Ted is a riot of stories. They tumble endlessly from him, and his bright-eyed, life-loving face leans towards me. His eyes spark in a joyous, inclusive conspiracy, and I am welcomed into the generous, irreverent world of his camaraderie, not a kid working a holiday, but a paid-up member of the rough-edged, comradely world of adult men.

Ted, Tiny, Arthur, Casper and the other men and boys of the Clements & Marshall shed stand luminous in the eye of memory. They are strong and welcoming and they turn a knowing, sardonic face to the world. Giant among them – I am being entirely literal – stands Jim Fulton, shed boss, Burnie football legend, driver in the Desert Campaign with the Rats. He is stern, kind and wise and he looks the other way when I disappear into the coolstore – as long as it is not plain to the eye that this case or that case is a couple of apricots the lighter for my visit. After the 1967 bushfires the ritual arrival of the truckload of apricots from the southern orchards is no more – and apricots have never since tasted as full of the flavour of the sun as those red-hearted Moorparks from the days before 'The Fires'. I learn – and have never forgotten – to tell at a glance whether a peach still groans with its picked freight of juice or whether its liquid spring has turned sere, leaving it mere dry pulp. I cannot tell you how I do it, but I'll bet I learnt it from Jim. I sit here now, with most that I will do with my life already in the ledger, and I try to calculate the debt I owe the men of the Clements & Marshall shed, and the brickyard, and the pea harvest, and I find the calculation beyond me.

Just half a dozen years on, armed with a Ph.D. and a job in Canberra, and home to visit family, on a whim I drive over to Jim's garden-girt house. Mrs. Fulton answers the door. I can no longer recall what she looked like – but I recall her words exactly. 'Oh he's dead, dear', she says. 'Yes, Jim's dead a while now.'

What constitutes 'good work'? Not such a difficult question. There is a veritable mountain of writing on the subject, and I've read quite a bit of it. Good work confers dignity on the doer, both because the work is intrinsically diverse, interesting and challenging, and because the outcome of the doer's labour is a product or service that adds to the good of the world. In the words of James Robertson, good work is 'activity which is purposeful and important'. Good work hones and satisfies the social life of a human. It conduces to autonomy, not dependence or disempowerment, and, as E.F. Schumacher so nicely put it, good work encourages 'the cultivation of a moral sensibility'. Whether, as a species, we have an ingrained need to work, period, is a more difficult question. Are we homo faber, the tools-wielding species that is denied its essence if denied work? Or is work a necessity that we must endure, even at its most satisfying, in order that we may meet the basic needs of life, preconditional to seeking the true development of our human potentialities within creative and recreational realms? This is a more difficult question, and it is not one I intend to ponder here – though it will become an imperative question, and will need an answer, in the decades ahead.

You would think, from the rhetoric, that all would be well. Today's buzzword, remember, is 'flexibility', and what comforting connotations of a fulfilling and creative workplace such a word evokes! Entirely illusory. Workplace 'flexibility' means insecure, casualised employment, with the heightened stress and anxiety that is the inevitable condition of an unsecured working future. No fulfilment in labour here, no enrichment of character, no responsibility, no joy in spontaneity, no development of a moral sensibility – because it is dog eat dog on the shop floor now, and the traits of character so cultivated are suspicion, aggression and toe-ragging, not sociality and fellow-feeling. Humiliation where there should be dignity. And, instead of autonomous, self-directing, engaged individuals, there is the normlessness of an abstract individualism. This is what you should read onto the page the next time you see such glib and facile slogans as 'workplace flexibility', or more specific synonyms for the same process like 'individual work contracts'. And I'm only talking here about the privileged West, you'll remember – yet most of the world's work is performed elsewhere and by women: and what Ariel Salleh has brilliantly termed the 'embodied materialism' of women's work is everywhere under *assault from the same ideological aggressors who are making over the nature of work in the West.*

Earlier I used the phrase — muttering darkly — 'they know not what they do'. And they don't. Francis Fukuyama is far from my favourite thinker, but he has a timely warning for the 'Nissan-chasers' — those who would abolish labour protection and drive down workplace standards in a dubious quest for freed-up investment. Fukuyama argues that capitalism can only work within a wider context of sociality. Market transactions, including those of the labour market, can never be effectively dehumanised. They depend crucially upon the maintenance of trust between people. And so it is that the disembodied capitalism envisioned by the fanatics of the new individualism will not work, because its dystopian wishfulness gets humans dismayingly wrong.

Technological and other forces have swept away the jobs I did in my holidays — though I suppose some storemen are still to be found in the sheds of the fruit and vegie wholesalers. Good riddance to the brickyard. But not the peas, and not the storeroom at Clements & Marshalls. There was much wrong with the way work was done there — on the pea harvest in particular. But they met many — even most — of the criteria for good work. I do not think most workplaces today could stand the comparison. Progress? You decide. I know what I think.

Not Far From Here: Thoughts on the Cataclysmic Art of Richard Wastell

(Written as the catalogue essay to accompany Richard Wastell's exhibition of the same name, in the Devonport Regional Gallery and the Dick Bett Gallery, January 2005. Richard's exhibition – brilliant work – was themed in large part on the destruction by fire of the windrowed debris of forest clearfells. The imagery in this poem/essay is taken from those artworks. The long [too long?] poetic excerpts are from 'Old Man's Beard', subsequently published in my collection, *Physick*, with the key difference that fire is transmogrified therein into ice!)

I go to the forests – not far from here. I enter worlds within worlds, worlds wheeling within and across each other, bleeding through boundaries, plunging down worm-holes of intricate life. Each world is an infinite, shape-shifting cosmos. It is so with colours, patterns, with process, with life itself, life as it plops and snarks in the leaf mould, as it winds and moles within snowgum bark. I know it random and chaotic; worlds of rioting spontaneity. I know it severe in its programmed constraint, ordered and gridded, an implausible geometry.

Such springing exuberance should be proof against destruction; too resilient. But so many of us come to it with hardened hearts; we do not see the small wheeling stars, the glorious reverence-commanding worlds, stretching ever down and away. We see a double-digit return to shareholders. We bring blades, chains, arc-lights, obliterating fires...

> *In the mountains*
> *post-noon*
> *night enters day.*

> *The air is a winding sheet*

> *for shamed*
> *wind-beaten peaks.*

> *The air is a rampant beast*
> *blackly rearing, huge,*
> *sun-blotting.*

I seek a hinge – a link from this ashed armageddon, its poisons and its charred grotesqueries, across to those lost, quick worlds, the tangled, fluid well of wonder that was here before the charrings, and before the desert of *nitens*. I wander, lost, past warped torsos of *Dicksonia antarctica*, stripped, black pillars of salt, void of feature. I reach from here to the redstreak bark of the snowgum, that blood-river that is the force of its life, and the forest's. That is my need.

To my mind comes the luminosity of lichen – Old Man's Beard – this concentrator, ramifier, of light within bush dark. It is my mind's hinge to the colours, the patterns, the razzmatazz of endlessly sunspotting life. Old Man's Beard.

> *The firestorm pends, is pent*
> *with light sucked from ligneous veins.*
> *And a marvel is here:*
> *these yellow scrags of lichen,*
> *scruffed entwined body hair*
>   *of the wind-twisted upland forest,*
> *these scrags restore the light.*

> *Old Man's Beard trims a lamp within too-early gloom.*
> *Here are crimped, soft strands,*
> *tangled finger-twists.*
> *They tease forth a fey and wondering light,*
> *the luminous calm of a gaze that falls upon the flawed nobility*
>   *of the acts of men,*
> *and the unimpeached dignity of the world on which they scrawl.*
> *Lichen is the forest's ancient enlightenment,*

> *and the planet's —*
> *and it reaches through the very fields of space*
> *to infuse the cosmic winds,*
> *a swirl of principle*
> *to spark a universe.*
>
> *And it swirls within, too,*
> *   to tap my animal soul,*
> *   to scatter firewalled fear,*
> *to welcome me,*
> *one of its elements, not alien,*
> *   a dancer in this clamorous, consuming moment,*
> *   this epic play of the world, of worlds.*

I am thinking of old bearded men with their 'crimped, soft strands' – of, say, old Philosopher Smith, the discoverer of the Waratah tin who opened the West Coast to mining – or their 'tangled finger-twists' of, say, marvellous old Walt Whitman. I am thinking of the thoughts of humans and the fate of the bush. One dreams a dream that leads straight to devastation; another dreams a different dream, a gentler dream, and the bush, too, dreams on, merely dreams on… I am thinking of the whirling arc of space and how it links to hard, precise mountain rock. Of colour hinged to dark. Of rampaging swirls of life hooked to grey wastes of death. Of the cosmos in the scale of a lake-caught trout or the red twist in a snowgum's bark within a blackened waste. And I need to know the point at which I am hooked in – not only to the yin of the surging life of the bush, but also to the yang of its visited death.

> *In the mountains*
> *   post-noon*
> *   light enters gloom,*
>
> *warms, is of,*

> *informs*
> *the soul of a world.*
>
> *I have my small share in it,*
> *world, light,*
> *idea,*
>
> *the old androgyne*
> *of the universe,*
> *its serum of wisdom,*
>
> *its principles of light,*
> *of dark,*
> *its finger-twists of lichen.*

The forest comes back. Every other writer of Letters-To-The-Editor tells me this. 'The forest grows back.' But it doesn't. Whatever comes back is not the forest that has gone. It may be in descent from that forest, but it grows on the far side of rupture. At best, now, there is a seam where once there was not – but nothing can be the same after rupture; certainly not after rupture as emphatic as this. Is it this realisation that leads me to seek solace in abstract principle, in the broad currents of change that transcend any one given clearfell?

It may be. Thanks to Old Man's Beard for its expansionary comfort, but it comes finally to this – there is no escaping the real, the tangible, the particular, and there is, then, no escaping the death of those myriad small worlds. Not far from here.

From a Suitcase in Maritime Canada

(First published in the American on-line journal, *Elsewhere*, in 2007. For the record, Alistair MacLeod died without ever making it to Tasmania.)

I was recently several weeks in Maritime Canada. My Tasmanian home naturally excepted, this is my favourite part of the planet, and I determined to write about it. This turned out to be easier said than done, and for two reasons.

First, I set out to write poetry — but I had been writing prose for too long, and the poetry metamorphosed into snippets of prose, the sort of thing that could have been called 'excerpts from a traveller's diary' — except that I didn't keep a diary. In a moment you'll read them.

The second reason was ideological. I had been reading about postcolonialism. I'm about to rehearse some arcane theory, but no need to panic. I'll be brief.

It is not possible to incontestably define 'postcolonialism', but I take it to refer to the persistence of certain ideologically-coded ideas, values and cultural processes that derive from past relationships of imperial dependency — which approximates the focus of Edward Said's seminal contribution to postcolonial theory. Leela Gandhi argues that such a definition plays up the self-importance of literary critics, because it enables 'postcolonial' to be defined principally as a cultural pathology. That's so - but, there is, I think, substance within the dross.

Anyway — there am I, a Tasmanian in Atlantic Canada, and there is no past relationship of dependency to implicate me here! But I know enough of the literature to recognize a postcolonial cast of mind — a sort of home-centred, prejudicial reflex — that can manifest whenever an artist engages creatively with a place, a culture, a society, and even a biota that is not the artist's own. I know this because, once my own island was 'discovered' in the mid 1990s as a suitably exotic literary backdrop, it was exploited in a series of acts of cultural appropriation that are well described as postcolonial plunder. This is what happens when a writer blows in to town on a flying visit (and sometimes not even that courtesy is paid), then proceeds to treat that place and its people as mere cliché, even bedecking the land with thoroughly alien flora and fauna, and making no attempt to engage with a complex and nuanced past and a complex and nuanced present. It is what happens when realworldness is treated with indifference; even contempt.

The Newfoundlanders already know this. Ask them what they think of The Shipping News, *then stand back. I determined that I would not be appropriatory in my own writing of Maritime Canada; that I would deal with other people's places respectfully and humbly, but from the undisguised perspective of an outsider. It can be done; Barry Lopez, a self-proclaimed 'writer who travels', manages it with ease. And here is what I came up with...*

*

These mid-May Nova Scotian woods. Can there be a more potent evocation of the utterly, the painfully, dreary? We are traversing the land at speed in a sealed and motorised can, and to the stood-off eye it is all spruced and sombre green and dead sticks, all a cutback blur from the highway's straight and functional line, and flat as the old tack. It badly wants the horizon-breaking jag of a mountain.

But step inside and here is the detail of wonder. A sly furl of life upon the ground. Pricked-green folds giving the lie to stick-death. The sudden polished plate of a lake's blue, moss-bound.

We pass a timber-getter's camp, his moonshine shack set aside by the stream. He emerges, middle-aged and big-gutted, all flannel-shirted and stubble-bearded suspicion. Now, I think, we're in for it. Then he speaks to us in French, and I know we're not. Johnny the Alsatian-cross dances in the stillness-after-rain. A nondescript shapelessness along the track cranks up his prancing excitement by several degrees, and now Johnny learns the woods' gothic corrective – his poor face is an arrow-quiver, pocked in porcupine quill.

*

Halifax. A gritty, on-the-edge town; elemental. The wind is sheer and blade-cold. Things happen here. Explosions. Planes down. And out beyond the conning-tower of that shore-cruising sub, a lump of ice once did for the world's greatest ship. Thousands have died. The wind, the sluicing wind, carries the breath of the thousands dead. Who could not love this town?

In the harbourside pub the music is as staunch as the town. The ghost of Stan Rogers, Canada's great troubadour, is here. *Now I'm a broken man on a Halifax pier, the last of Barrett's privateers.* There is a tight-topped girl shimmering in a roil of tough male lust. Hard young men, holding to a forced and fraying camaraderie. The joust for Fair Lady's favour wheels and eddies, favourites come, favourites go. We get a skin-blistering blast of Great Big Sea. *Can't make nuthin out of nuthin, give my country back its heart.* The tight-topped girl ripples a wave and leaves alone. Who could not love this town?

My Haligonian host is gentler than his town. He installs me in an old and doddering fisherman's shack. Later I say, jocular old me, 'I suppose the shanty would have to be haunted'. Not a twitch at the edge of the mouth. Not a hint of play in the line of the eye. His face is the deadest of pans as he says, 'didn't you wake in the night certain there was a face an inch away, staring into your own?'

Prosaic, unfey me. What a disappointment I am. 'Slept like a gin-fed babe', I lie.

*

In the Bonshaw Hills the May sun bites, brings endless greens in its train, and startling yellows. There is a skunk beneath the shed.

The island's great fiddler sits in shade on the bank. His angularity sketches a jack-knifed, 10-past-four geometry. He plays a waltz with no name. 'Y'learn a tune from some other fuhla', he says, 'but y'never learn its name. Yuh ask the other fiddlers, y'say, do yuh know the name of this? And it's "nuh", "nuh", "nuh"'. He has a smile like the broad curve of the North Shore. I lean against the shed, warm with sun and Lagavulin. Not enough space for the skunk to cock its tail.

There's a three-legged coyote about. I look, knee-jerk foolish, to the woods. Coyotes are recent arrivals – they crossed the winter sea-ice just a few short years ago. 'People lose their cat', says our host, 'and it's likely the coyote.' He pronounces 'coyote' in the conventional way, but that seems unusual. Down east last week, and even at last night's lobster supper, it was 'kai-yoat'.

Whatever it answers to the coyote out there in the woods wants for a leg, but he still has my host worried. There's his much-loved dog, Molly. Molly enters the fourth hour of 'throw the ball at the shed and I'll git it'. She is inexhaustibly canine, and without a thought for the Lurker at the Threshold, the three legged Thing from the demi-world. 'Porcupines on the island?', I ask. 'Nuh.'

The great fiddler idly plucks and strums, launches into a wild and raunchy 'Summertime', stops mid-chord to throw the ball for Molly. Later we drive through a North Shore dusk. There are foxes, flame-tailed and brazen, in the fields, even on the road's verge. This is a new and strange thing, and there's a theory:

Kai-yoat has won the woods and driven old Tod to the fields, to the open country. I take a close look at old embattled Tod. He is all tail, but there is no bounce to it, no shine to his coat, and his face is pocked and scarred. I am sure I see desperation in his eyes.

The echo of the devil's jig hovers in the dusk.

*

I meet an artist who looks like Eric Bogle. His work is on show, tricked out to take the eye. I see lush island pastorals, Anne of Green Gables' saccharine legacy in another predictable manifestation.

Wait, though. The girls in sweet flounces have hard, implacable eyes. And there – look – there too, hints of weirdly-cast evil skitter in the shrubbery, in the doll's house, hideously there through the spokes of the perambulator. There is a worm at work, and it is not benign.

The artist's face is benign. And his easy, intelligent talk. Here in this island of churches his main living is to be found in the vivid brilliance of stained ecclesiastical glass. He is said to be a Druid.

Some functionary bustles through the hall, bristling with detail and import. He snaps my conversation with the Druid mid-sentence, ignores me, launches into a complexly imperious set of instructions. He breaks his bombast only long enough to say, 'do you have any questions?' The Druid who works in worm and sanctified glass says, 'what is the capital of Albania?'

*

The Newfies hate 'Newfie', but they shouldn't – just as we Vandiemonians shouldn't hate the perennial mainlander 'show us the scar on your shoulder' so-called joke. And so...

At the Charlottetown Wine Festival a kind and dapper Newfie, dark and crinkle-eyed, dispenses Australian plonk.

It's a grand, cosmopolitan swirl. Stalls of vintaged exotica proclaim Chile, Spain, California, France, Argentina, Italy, South Africa, Portugal and, well, Canada. And Australia. I look for patriotic surprises, find none. These are the too-familiar, high-volume lines that, back home, you only ever buy on special. The vinous products of global capital, muscled in through corporate takeover. Though I wish it were not so, they are also, by some margin, the best plonk here.

The man from Newfoundland dispenses my country's plonk with flair; with a confident authority. His spiel is oiled, polished, sad. When, all tipsy arrogance, I play the 'bullshit-I-come-from-there' card, he abandons the farce with manifest relief. 'My uncle went t'Melbourne after he married bad', he tells me. 'Even his in-laws warned him against her.' 'So', I ask, 'how does he like it there?' 'He jumped off a cliff', says the kind, smiley-eyed Newfie. Then he salts the silence. 'But *she's* still alive'.

The dark and crinkled man from Corner Brook pours another transnational Australian red. 'Git yr laughin gear around that', he says, accent perfecto.

*

Sea Cow Pond is a landlocked bubble with a run to the sea.

There is a legend and it is this: the Malpeque Scots, Macdonalds all, and starving in that first iced-in winter, are coasted along by the Mi'kmaq to this old walrus haul-out. Thus are they saved. The lord is duly praised and down in Nova Scotia, General Amherst and Governor Cornwallis plan the dispensation of pox-ridden blankets to that 'execrable race', the Mi'kmaq.

In 2003 a sea cow hauls out on Cape Breton's *Fleur-de-lis* shore. It is properly admonished. 'Over a thousand miles from home', shouts the fourth estate. That far, eh? Get ye gone.

There is a M. Doucette at Sea Cow Pond. He idles benignly by the boat-lined sea-bubble, overalled, ruddy and wide-smiled. 'They's all this asthma on the island', he says, 'all that sprayin uv the spuds. Course, y'can't prove nuthin.' He stands next to a lobster boat, plane-shaving lined, the abrupt brown-eye of a stern naming it the 'I Hate Fishin'. 'This yours?', I want to ask. I wish him instead a bland nice day, and he responds: 'Oh, I'm after cuttin a cord a red maple, down back aways.'

In Charlottetown I tell this story, and I'm told, 'most likely he lost his womenfolk t'cancer. They die in their thirties up there, y'know.'

*

I drive the northwest coast with a folklorist, a small and brilliant man with a different tale for every revolution of the wheel. Last summer he pulled a human skeleton from the cliff over there, and this not the first. Male, very tall, head pointed west, arms crossed over breast, the remains of a coffin. A mystery. 'There's no record of a burial ground there', he says, 'and after about 1820 there wus a perfectly good Presbyterian graveyard just down the shore. So this had t'be an earlier site. Or a burial from a single disaster – and it's sure enough there's a killer reef just out there'. Was the skeleton taken away to be dated? 'Nuh. Just buried down there in the cemetery.'

We head inland, to potato country. Here is the economic heart of 'Spud Island', but it is a diseased heart, and the discourse shifts. 'Look at these huge fields. The hedgerows have gone, the hedgerows that give cover for weasels and muskrats and such. But people are wising up. Y'know, the environment is the big sleeper out here. Look that way. Y'can see for two miles and not a hedgerow. The topsoil y'know, it just blows away in the dry without the hedges. Twenty years ago that would uv been a quilt of fields with hedgerows, maybe eight fields in there...'

*

Here is a day of high summer, a day of humming-birds and subversion.

The Friday beer-drinkers talk electoral reform. I disgrace myself: I'd rather watch the humming-birds. 'Well it's fine for you', I think but do not say. 'In Tasmania we don't have life so liquid-in-air.'

I go to talk politics at Catholic Family Services. My host is a third cousin once removed of Mary MacKillop. 'They's MacKillops over on Cape Breton still', she says, 'if y'care t'look'. She is spare, feisty and getting on and she takes no prisoners. Patronage in government gets thoroughly junked. This is a lively conversation between kindred souls, but I choose words carefully – a come-from-away is only as good here as the cut of his next sentence. There is a poster on the wall and it says:

> WHEN I GIVE FOOD TO THE POOR
> THEY SAY I'M A SAINT.
> WHEN I ASK WHY THE POOR HAVE NO FOOD
> THEY SAY I'M A COMMUNIST.

Two humming-birds at a feeder is fifty percent too much humming-bird. How can a bird the size of a bumblebee freight so much fight? Its wings are an air-stalling blur, its temperament all cock. It is a jewel strapped to a miniature rudderless rocket.

*

'We were goin t'make it a stook, but the old fuhla ran out of twine'. That's the punchline of a story. Here they tell stories as public entertainment. Make your own story to put above that punchline.

The story-teller considers his art. 'The language comes up from the soil. I would listen to these big, strong men with poetry on their tongue. I do what I do because I'm afraid we'll lose the metaphors, lose the beauty in the particulars of the language. These days technological language is universal...'

This island is connected to New Brunswick by a bridge. A bloody big bridge. When you cross it, though, you get no sense of crossing a bridge. The parapet is deliberately designed to deny a view. There is no dramatic climb and descent. It is just another road, really. When is an island not an island...

'MOOSE', say the signs by the road; and 'DEER'. The road is littered with sad huddled bundles that once were porcupine. Well at least that tells me I'm off the island. To my shame the signage intrigues more than this northern New Brunswick landscape.

>   CAP-PELÉ
>   Au Coeur de l'Acadie
>
>   Donna's Folk Art
>
>   Ye Must Be Born Again
>   PREPARE TO MEET THY LORD
>
>   Autoroute des anciens combattants
>
>   Fred's Boulangerie

('Fred's Boulangerie'! Next time I'm asked to define multiculturalism I'll just say 'Fred's Boulangerie'!)

FRENCHY'S
FAMILY CLOTHING CENTRE
CLOSED FOR THE SEASON
THANK YOU

There is an election in New Brunswick this week. If the employment stats are anything to go by this is an economy in rags. But just yesterday my own island was awash with unqualified enthusiasm for 'the New Brunswick Model'. Then a whimsical political breeze flipped the 'Model' off the platform, and it was lost... And I am here pondering the inkling of a theory to do with the economic multiplier of an IT economy, or why there might not be one...

We reach Moncton and my carseat depression is consummated. Moncton is a tidal bore (read that as you will) and one vast carpark for a shopping mall. I look back down the long road travelled, across the bridge that is merely a road, and I see a ragged trail of metaphor, the poetry of an island living, waiting in line to pay the toll. *'We were goin t'make it a stook, but the old fuhla ran out of twine'.*

When is an island not an island...

*

This was a day on the island...

In the morning I stroll a fieldpath to a tree-enclosed square. Flowers nod me along – vetch, hawkweed, devil's paintbrush. I am puffy with immature pride – that I should be able to show-off like this, putting names to flowers of the fields and forests of a distant land.

Red stumps stud the little square, and I think of a giant's rotten teeth. It is a small square of death, an old graveyard. For thirty years it gathered in the island pioneers, then closed to begin a quick return to the red and shapeless earth. Except that, in 1851, when the Yankee Gale howled, and 80 schooners out of Nova Scotia and the 'Boston States' drove their bows under wave and shore, this little square opened its red doors once more to accept the gift from the Yankee Gale. The wind howled as it has never howled, the sea rose to the drumming deathsong, and the island's cradled shore took the sad jetsam, North Cape to East Point, unto itself.

Just where the men of Massachusetts lie in this pocket of earth cannot be known, not here, not in any of the little North Shore squares bossed with shape-worn lumps of red. So many dead. This should be the great island-shaping myth, but is not. My thought is ungenerous but irresistible: it is because these were men from away, these doomed seekers after mackerel. But I try to be fair. I think: 'I suppose that matters – that they were not island men.'

I leave the square, the path coloured up with devil's paintbrush, and the sun, out here, is an egg-fryer. Impossible on such a day to enchant the facts of history. How high the seas? How wild the wind? I cannot bring the Yankee Gale into poetry's livingness, and I seem to hear the dead cry at my back, to call upon me the shame of the absorbed here, the traitorous now.

In the afternoon I am on a trail in the woods. I have brought Longfellow along. All these years on and he finally walks here – well, not on Evangeline's Bay of Fundy shore perhaps, but at least within the Maritime woods. And he is good enough to declaim the great line on cue: *Still stands the forest primeval.* From roots twined deep he has fetched a sighing refrain on the popular breath.

The trouble is – he is wrong. The fields and forests are in perpetual exchange. They are island chessmen: field takes forest takes field takes forest. It is a joust between machines and the white spruce. Look, though, at a field 'going spruce' and you'll know what tomorrow brings. The spruce is alert, explosive fecundity, and in this light-repellant gloom, just here, it is no easy remembrance that, a turn of the trail away, spruce-nurtured birches curtsy with light, buttered slabs of it here, tweaked slats of it there. Even the ailing beech, perhaps, might, when we are gone, be gentled back.

I nod to Longfellow with a new respect. Machines are at their sorry work as I write, but the green surge is *primeval,* and on it sparks, on and on... Greens glide into infinite greens, and even in spruce-gloom there is sparkle where the brush-soft quills of new growth dance at the membrane of light. The tree startles and shifts to a realm beyond language, its outstraining impulse to life travelling through knotted dark to the concentrated small light of fingertips. It is a joyful chant in the unheard voice of a music of silence, whole to itself, unforced, unshaped by subtle tactic, a master piece for wind, light and life, made for itself, the idea of an audience absurd.

It is music inexorable, rolling out to encompass the world.

And now, in the evening, I enter Bingo Country. I survey cheap trestles and a basic box stage and prepare for anything.

I get a man in check flannel and workboots and a storm-gouged face that dances to a spring of joy, a benevolence that enfolds us in uncomplicated warmth. In his vast and ugly hands he holds a pair of spoons, and he waits on a stool on the stage, those huge knobbled hands covering his knees as he beams delight upon Bingo Country, now peopled with long-loved school friends, the 80-year olds of the island.

I get him – and I get, too, winsome sweetness in a ponytail and tight, excruciating bands of adolescent timidity. In her hand she holds a bow and fiddle, and talk is the hardest thing in the world — but talk she must because this is her show, and she will be calling the shots.

Now one reeboked foot smashes against the makeshift stage — and again, and again... And the wild ache of the years — hundreds of them — that have made her, and the music, and the old man with the spoons, and all the tired and groaning limbs in the audience this night, explodes through her fiddle in a shout of exile and rebirth that clamours about the dark and cobwebbed corners of Bingo Country. The ponytail twirls to the reel, and the bow drags from the strings a cry of mystery and love and hope and loss that taps the stream of life itself — and death — and the spoons clatter as deft and as sure as bones, and the reeboked foot, wild, remorseless, slams on upon the stage. The 80-year olds strew the night with tattoos of mid-performance applause. They cheer the girl and the man, yes, but they cheer, too, this small sign that their life will persist, that it will flow on into that dangerous time to come when they will be gone.

Later a step-dancer's flying feet strike the excitement along. She is, maybe, 15. An aged voice behind me says, 'that will uv run the beer out uv her'. But the voice is no fit to the words. It floats through Bingo Country with a light and tender love, and into the softened air of an island night.

*

The sun is in the wrong place. My directional radar — a reliable, well-tuned instrument — is out of kilter. Everything is counter-intuitive. Okay. I can work with that. We are on the west coast of Cape Breton Island. The *Boston States* are at my back. We are going *down north*. Even a *come-from-away* copes.

The houses are beautiful. We had this fine vernacular knowhow back home once. We, too, moulded exquisite habitat in timber; then, inexplicably, we gave it up. These houses catch the breath. They sit in springing green meadow, no fences, rarely a garden.

We move from Acadien towns to towns of Scots Gaelic – well, some still have the *auld* tongue – in the space of a road's curve. But we are tourists – we do not see the gutted communities. We do not see the closed and blighted mines, the body-crippling, widow-making mines. We do not see the despair, the slow down-the-years anger.

Here is Mabou, the Nashville of Cape Breton fiddle, music touched with a holy fire. We visit – he is just up the road – 'down north' – the great author, Alistair MacLeod. Is there, I ask myself, a finer living exponent of the short story? No, I conclude, there is not. Alistair is a sweet and generous man; too generous by far with the *wusgee*. His novel has just won the Whitbread. 'What's next, Alistair?', asks the brash, unworldly Tasmanian. 'Next', says the great man, fencing behind the smile, 'next I'm coming to Tasmania'.

The land rears at the sky. After all that Nova Scotian flatness, the land rears at the sky. Here in the fastnesses of these upland forests it may be that the considered-extinct eastern cougar still holds on. I'm a Tasmanian: there is thylacine *mythos* in my blood and the story of the cougar fires me up. The locals shrug their shoulders.

We trek the National Park. On the upland barrens the vegetation is razored off at a height above my head. The moose do that. The vast upland is a moose hedge. There are bears, too, but these are black bears 'and they won't hurt yuh. Moose, though, y'meet a moose on the trail, y'watch his feet, not all that superstructure on his head. It's the hooves that'll do for yuh.'

It's been a grand, mooseless day. We're in a roadhouse, eating lobster. I'm scanning the local paper, reading how yesterday a trekker in these parts was mauled to death by a black bear.

*

There you have my traveller's vignettes, all of them arrant failures. My attempt to be non-appropriatory, to write from the vantage of a sympathetic, even enthusiastic outsider, has flopped utterly. Instead of empathetic outsideness I have adopted a mean tone, judgemental, and the affection in which I hold the people of whom I write has morphed into smartarsedness (as we would put it hereabouts).

This happened, I think, because I found it impossible to suspend tacit comparison with my own much-loved place.

Lopez, who so successfully achieves where I have failed, always travels with an informed insider. For the most part, so did I. But I knew the places I visited only subjectively – not with the objective understanding that comes from an immersed, time-rich experience. I am impatient with people who claim, after a five-minute acquaintance, that here is the place for them; that they have found 'home' – as I am with people who claim the whole planet for 'their' place. Impossible. Until you know how non-human life moves through and within a place, until you have a deep vernacular acquaintance with its realms of story, until you unselfconsciously read the play of the elements as they unfold through the day and through the year, until you know how great geological forces have worked away through deep time, until you know how humans have interacted with each other and with the elements of that place – until then you are not truly at home. Most people, even those with generational ties to a place, cannot claim this. That is why placelessness is such a rampant modern pathology.

A writer is, of course, perfectly entitled to write of any place under the sun. It is not the legitimacy of the enterprise per se that is in dispute. But within the undertaking lurk unanticipated traps for the unwary. It is no easy thing to write successfully of not-one's-place. Protocols apply, and I have violated them.

My rendering of direct speech, for example. I hear my protagonists saying those things exactly as I have written them. But they themselves will think that I have made them sound like Americans, and will feel duly aggrieved. And an Australian reader will think my rendering remarkably similar to our own vernacular. Fair comment. Then there are those fluffy punchlines. They read now as substitutes for an honest engagement with place and people. And as for my alien's descriptions of the landscape of northern New Brunswick, and even the Nova Scotian interior — what a failure of empathetic imagining these represent, for there are folk who call these biologically and historically rich landscapes home, and who are attached to them as powerfully as I am to Tasmania. I owe them an apology.

Some vignettes almost work. I get closest in the three stages of that single busy day observed in the narrative that begins 'This was a day on the island...'. Except that the description of the ceilidh in Bingo Country uncomfortably resembles what is, to my mind, the high point of Tasmanian literary achievement, the extraordinary 'Aboriginal band in the Dog House' sequence in Richard Flanagan's Death of a River Guide. *And except that I am inexcusably ungenerous in the description of my visit to the old cemetery on Prince Edward Island's North Shore — the Yankee Gale rumination. There is diamond in the dross only in my description of the trail through the spruce forest; only there, and only briefly, does ambition meet achievement in engagement with a not-my-own-place.*

One swallow, as it is said, does not a summer make. My Canadian writings remain failures, and I have learned a lesson — to stay within the narrow range of my competence. To deploy another bon mot, *one rarely heard these days, 'the cobbler should stick to his last'!*

Defending the Wild Lands

(An earlier version of this essay was published in *Endangered: Tasmania's Wild Lands* [Penguin 2007].)

This is the island at the end of the earth.

Beyond the blue cut of its horizons the world is winding down, buckling under the weight we have pressed upon it. Irresponsible governments, captive to the money and the flattery of the powerful, are responsible for much of that weight. We consumers, obsessively guzzling, gorging and discarding, are responsible for much of the rest. The doctrines that sanction these pathologies are articles of faith to the most powerful men (they are usually men) and institutions on the planet.

What does it mean to stand upon the island at the end of the earth and gaze out at the mad heedlessness of this, the last of the exuberant times?

First, it is to view the planet from a comparatively uncluttered vantage point. As the world 'globalises', its political, economic and cultural variety rendered down, its riotous anarchy displaced by a single integrated system, it may be from the geographical outriggers that the expropriatory nature of this grey and uniform world is most clearly discerned.

Second, it is to recognise the *value* of this island. It is to look upon a world enduring rapid impoverishment on all dimensions except that which is most illusory and of least import – the economy of the moment – and to know that here there are still blue skies and star-studded nights, clean air and water, fish in the sea, forests (with mammals in them), trees (with birds in them), mountains untamed, time and space, wonder, mystery, magic, spirit. It is to know that this is an island like no other, an island complete unto itself, with a dark and turbulent recent past belonging to this island only. Most of us at least understand it to be a special place without, perhaps, quite knowing why.

That 'dark and turbulent' past is the 200-year old shadow that lurks at our shoulder, but spin on your heel, look back, and it slips away. The shadow of our unconfronted past is at the heart of an unreconciled collective psyche. But a past of dark and unreconciled deeds does not make us special. The recently departed century – the century of war – spattered the planet with atrocity and abomination. The island's unique quality is not to be found here.

Where, then? The island's graceful colonial architecture, perhaps, still sufficiently extant to potently project the past into the present. But somewhere in the middle years of the last century we lost interest in maintaining a distinctive architectural tradition and embraced instead the placeless design principles and building technologies that signify a global sameness. Our built places are rapidly becoming one with Provincetown and Smallville the world over.

If not its built form, then, what of its people? This, I think, is what most people would want to claim as the source of the island's distinctiveness. I agree, though only up to a point. There *is* a distinctiveness about the island's people. Its rural folk, especially in the north, still speak an old bush argot in that strong and broad tonal inflection that has vanished from much of Australia. They retain, many of them, an allegiance to old values of decency, reciprocity, fellow-feeling and comradeship that are viewed with lip-curling scorn by the go-getters of corporate Australia. More nebulous – but more auspicious – is the claim, most conspicuously made by Richard Flanagan, that there is enough in its store of transmitted story and culture, the particular histories the island's children absorb through the pores of their skin, the character of life here experienced – an elusive Tasmanian 'cast' – to warrant a claim for Tasmania as 'another country'. The case is well made, and I subscribe to it – but it is possible to make too much of this. To the north sits a large island with which Tasmania shares, in large part, institutions, economic fortune and misfortune, substantial cultural commonality, recreational interests and passions, partisan political configurations, myth constructions, life aspirations, and very much more. Even that wonderful old speech survives in parts of the big island to the north; so does the wry, storied way of discourse, and those embattled values of communality and other-regarding compassion also cling tenaciously on. And there are, here in the island at the end of the earth, venal, mean-spirited, immoral, murderous, racist, exploitative, debased, two-faced, callous, conscience-free bastards in pretty much the same proportions as there are throughout the earth. Tasmanians are different then, but not so very different – the claim for the island's especialness to reside within its people, then, can only be partly made.

There is a third contendor, and there will be no prizes for divining what it is.

Tasmania is a wet and temperate island. It is lush, green, robust. Its terrain is broken into serrated ridgelines, arêtes, moraines and mountains, all punctuated by sudden lakes, tarns, driving creeks and boggy, tussock-pocked plains, all of which is stitched together by a bewildering tangle of vegetation, the types and communities of which shift with startling frequency.

Here, I think, is the clue to the island's call upon its people's commitment, passion and mobilisation for action. It lies in the land. The island's definitive qualities, the core qualities that we might call its soul – are the biophysical currents that shape life in *all* its forms. They are the still older, imperceptible but implacable geological processes that will one day decree the island to have had its day. And they are the forms of life, in all their boisterous variety (human included), that have co-evolved, through deep tides of time, with the island itself. You want the essence of Tasmanian soul, distinction, transcendent value? You must look to the wild land. It is there. And much follows from this.

*

I am in the Kodama Forest in the Blue Tier. Above me is a dusty forest road, and an untenanted space that was once the briefly vibrant tin town of Lottah. The Tiers are an unplotted maze of shafts, diggings and other slow-rotting artefacts of the mining days. But here below the Lottah Road I am in a small defile of stately, mature tree ferns (*Dicksonia antarctica*), their fronds shivering above a quiet, deep-breathing forest hall. There are people gathered here. Many are local activists, members of Friends of the Blue Tier, but some are Japanese students from the University of Tasmania. We are to hear and read poetry, and there are Japanese translations of poetry written for the occasion, fluttering on tasselled ribbons from frond and sprig. A hale breeze blows, and it penetrates even this sheltered hollow, setting up a tinkling soundscape from the strings of bells with which the grotto has been festooned. In the damp mould by a faint creek line threading the grove, a Japanese water harp has been installed. The ancient green of Gondwana and the trance-inducement of the soft ripple of bells dissolve the bounds of time. It is a special place and it can be nowhere else on earth – but it connects me to the special that is in all the Earth, affirming the futility of xenophobic place meanings, scoping my sympathies, my responsibilities, globally.

And now I am walking in the heat and steam of dry sclerophyll forest on Bruny Island. A combination of rain and sun has released a delicate sweetness from the forest and life has danced abroad. It is a celebration of the pure, marvellous fact of *is*. It is in the canopy, where a carillon of birdsong trills flawless, intricate movements of the bush's symphony for infinite voice. It is on the ground, where echidna fixes me with a droll eye, twitches its pike-armoured back and waddles away. There are tiger snakes everywhere, their glide all fluid grace. The thud of apprehension that customarily accompanies their sudden presence is absent today – they are benign with the glory of the day. I examine the abstract masterpieces of bark-sap-insect patterns on tree trunks, 'Self Portrait' by *E. viminalis,* and *E. viminalis* has a palette of such delicate mauve, smoke, pink, green-tinge, indigo, rust, cream, olive and lemon that it defies reproduction. But even this, I know, is a façade; mere surface show for a whole hidden world within a world, one of utter, marvellous complexity...

So might a writer write of the wild places. It is a perspective from aesthetics – according to my dictionary, 'the science of the beautiful'. Fact yields to feeling, to impression, to spontaneity, allusion, poetry, suggestion, wonder, epiphany, even rapture – though a grounded, worldly rapture. Artists working in other modes, photography, say, will deploy the same expressive priorities.

Those who take a camera and an artist's eye into the wild lands do so, I presume, for a variety of reasons, though certain features will recur. In my view the collective enterprise loosely labelled 'wilderness photography' is the most distinctively Tasmanian artform, though it is one that has had to wear criticism. Tasmanian 'wilderness' photography, it is held, conspires in the fiction that the wild places are devoid of people. The myth is sustained that, in the absence of any human defilement, the wild places are more 'pure' and, thus, 'precious'. The second is that Tasmanian wilderness photography seeks to portray an unremitting beauty, thereby narrowing its aesthetic range and screening from our perception such qualities as danger, death, decay, terror, predatoriness, though these are every bit as characteristic of life in the wild — perhaps even more so — than lyrically arrayed beauty. A variation on this criticism is that Tasmanian wilderness photography seeks shamelessly to manipulate our sensibilities, to bedazzle and seduce; a form of 'eco-porn'.

I think these criticisms miss the point, though I'll set the first aside and consider only a single aspect of the second here. Speaking personally, when it comes to visual communication I want most to experience that which inspires; that which will renew the passions of my engagement with the island. There is a political point to wilderness photography, then. It is to affirm commitment and strengthen resolve. And it also has an aesthetic purpose. Photographers are visual poets of the wild world. The effects they seek are the effects that poets seek.

There are alternative ways of comprehending the wild, but I want to assert the particular validity of aesthetic understandings of the wild places. Why should it be, I wonder, that 'beauty', 'love', 'inspiration' get such a bad press? What a middle-class luxury must a concern for aesthetic quality and other 'ephemera' be, runs one prominent argument, when so many people lack the basics. Consider, though, this argument that only the privileged have the requisite sensibility to respond to the beautiful and the inspiring. How class-prejudicial is that? In my experience anyone, no matter where they sit at the unequally-furnished table of material goods, is capable of response to the intangible values of place and nature. Only those middle-class paternalists who claim to speak for the less well-off on the ground that such people have no capacity to do this themselves could blithely perpetuate such an insult. Do manual workers want to live in a dismal, dehumanising, grey and monotonal world? I think not. No, then, this is not a class issue.

There is another good reason why aesthetics matter. An aesthetic sensibility correlates in large part with an ethical one. The absence of the one correlates with the absence of the other. Both sensibilities remove you from self-absorption to contemplation of larger issues of justice, wellbeing, truth, of the 'oughts' of life. They engender fellow feeling for that which is different; to know how it, he or she sees itself. It is for this reason that most people who are passionate about social justice are also passionate about environmental justice – and vice versa. It is for this reason that the voices of artists and those in the 'human professions' figure prominently against the callous treatment of those who lose in the shake-out: refugees, single mums, structurally displaced labour, animals, forests…

*

This will become clearer if we go where the photographers have gone. We could go to the Arthur-Pieman on the clamorous West Coast, into coastal dune country, a vast Aboriginal midden of such incalculable import that it merits World Heritage protection. We would find no such protection; we would find the epitome of management ineptitude and the systematic trashing of irreplaceable Indigenous heritage by unconstrained 4WD activity and by deliberate, calculated atrocity.

We could move through the West Coast mineral belt – carefully excluded from the World Heritage Area when the boundaries of the latter were drawn: because in this scheme of official value, mining trumps World Heritage – and there we might catalogue the scars forged by those who go in search of the next briefly incandescent mineral boom. It is not difficult to find evidence of the subservient status of values intrinsic to wildness when it comes to extractive economics, or energy generation, or high-impact recreation. But let us instead climb a mountain road into the tiers to the east of Launceston, up to the headwaters of the

North Esk River. Up the Camden Road with Ben Nevis on our right shoulder, and into the Camden Forest.

Into a clearfell.

*

It is one thing to be endlessly lyrical. It is one thing to craft imagery (by word, by photo) of what is special, unique, of inestimable value within this wondrous island. That is all that should be needed. For it is surely not even comprehensible that people – Tasmanians, at that – would deliberately set out to destroy the rich manifestations of glorious life that hold the island's soul. It is surely not comprehensible that calculated violence would be actively *promoted* by a government that holds a steward's charge over the island's vital biophysical processes. Oh yes it is.

It is hard to explain a clearfell to those who have never stood within the slaughtered heart of a dismembered, firebombed forest. Those who have done this customarily deploy 'ground zero' language. Dresden and Hiroshima are invoked; sometimes more conventional battleground imagery. I have used it myself, though the truth is that, given its association with the utter extremes of horror that humans can inflict upon other humans, I am somewhat uneasy about it. The trouble is, without recourse to battleground imagery it is very difficult to find comparative points of reference that can evoke an approximate mental image. But I'll try.

Here was forest: a breathing, complex mesh of living relationships. Those myriad intricate worlds – those worlds within worlds with their snark and their snuffle – are all gone; obliterated entirely. Colour, pattern, process – individual units of life and chaotic worlds of rioting spontaneity – gone. The springing exuberance of these entangled, time-sculpted worlds should be proof against destruction; too resilient. But people come who do not see the small, intricate worlds stretching down and away forever, nor even do they see, for that matter, the larger world that is the forest itself, though it is right there for the seeing. They see, instead, a burgeoning bottom line. They bring instruments of destruction. They wage war on behalf of death.

This is the process. First, the forest is smashed apart; razed to the ground. It may be that some small pockets are left standing. In the weasel words of the times this is now referred to as 'selective logging' – a cynical misuse of a term that once referred to logging regimes that left a forest's structure intact. Then the dead forest is shunted into windrows. Then it is napalmed. The storm of fire smoulders down to an ashed armageddon, a boneyard of grotesque torsos, charred and twisted shapes as void of feature as the shadows of hell.

There is a decisive hinge between the thoughts of humans and the fate of the forests. Someone dreams thus, and that is what happens. Another might dream a gentle dream and the forest might be spared to dream its own dreaming. None of it is inevitable – we can choose the dream we want. One dream leads to grey wastes of death, to the panoramic sweep of a monochromed wasteland. But this is the dream of those in power.

We are witnessing in the Tasmanian forests the triumph, total to the point of totalitarian, of the anti-values of technocracy. Maximised production, the greatest output from the least possible input, is the rule, and all other values are swept away before the single cause of maximised technical efficiency. It is the triumph of process over consequence, of the how over the what and the why. Decision-making is distilled to questions of technique and procedure, politics is pared down to a narrow range of technical options, and questions pertaining to more fundamental matters are screened out; stripped of legitimacy. That is why dissenting voices within debates over the future of the forests are not heard within government. It is because those voices are not asking technical questions. As far as those with political and economic power are concerned, they are not asking *relevant* questions.

I saw this dramatically demonstrated a few short years ago when I attended a public appeal against a planned local forest operation, the declaration of a Private Timber Reserve. It was an appeal that was not supposed to have been possible, because the drafters of the Act had drastically constrained legal standing, virtually eliminating all potential grounds for appeal. After all, if decisions are merely technical in nature, and the preserve of an elite with access to the requisite technical skills, why should an ignorant public be given a say? Only through the tenacity and ingenuity of an articulate local community was the matter reluctantly permitted to proceed to appeal. At the hearing several local people attested to the likely impact upon their place values and other semi-tangible amenity factors. When he rose to cross-examine these witnesses, the representative of Private Forests Tasmania largely ignored all this, asking instead a series of detailed scientific questions, the point of which was to demonstrate the technical illiteracy of the local witnesses. Having made his point he didn't even bother to draw his conclusion. Not necessary. Game, set and match.

We are back with science. The technocrat denies legitimacy to all discursive paradigms but one. All validity is invested in something called 'science'. But what I want to know is: whose science? There is not a single 'seamless' science, but a series of scientific value-sets, hedged about with assumptions inherent in the very *purpose* of the chosen scientific endeavour. Wildlife scientists are not just working on different problems to Monsanto's geneticians or NASA's aeronautical engineers; they are very different scientists, with different working assumptions, different conceptions of what constitutes good scientific practice, and different notions of what it is that science needs to know and upon which it should be focused. All expertise is partial, then, hedged about by the focus of the expert's training and by the value paradigm – the ideology – that clings potently to any 'brotherhood' of expertise. Forestry scientists are trained within a specific and constrained range of expertise, and they work within a defined set of values that constitutes a professional ideology, one that is not shared by many scientists with somewhat similar expertise derived from the study of the natural world. In the island at the end of the earth, then, there are biogeographers, botanists, ecologists, zoologists and hydrographers who reject a very great deal of what passes for official forestry science.

At stake is a fundamental clash of values: technocrats who look at the forest and see mere 'resource', valueless in any terms other than dividend and export dollar, against those who look at the forests and see the living soul of the land. Those of us in the latter camp spend our lives in a grey fog of grief. It is real grief, and unlike the grief experienced at the death of someone dear, it is never assuaged, because it goes on and remorselessly on. With every forest that is ripped apart the island is irreparably diminished in the sensibilities of those who love it for what it is – and its people are diminished with it.

*

No mere management solution, one dedicated to the constrained vision of maximising efficient extraction, can bring an end to the harsh politics of the forests. Only a measured reduction in the scale of the timber industry, a return to a social forestry, labour- and sawlog-intensive, and oriented to local need can achieve that. A forestry small in scale, the sort that was envisaged by those who naively called for a plantation-based industry two decades ago, thinking that an industry of that modest scope, one deployed upon farmlands of marginal productivity, would be the saviour of the primal forests. No-one imagined back then an industry of such magnitude or such insatiable rapacity, one that came to say 'plantations it is – and to make way for those plantations every forest that has not been accorded some form of reserve status becomes a candidate for clearing'.

Opinion polls consistently show that 70 percent and more of Tasmanians want forest clearance to end, but the complexities that determine voting behaviour have not turned such opinion into votes. So government, in thrall to vested industrial interests, hangs tough, and the system is sealed from the public to the very limit of possibility. Forestry operations are exempted from the state's planning system. Its codes of practice are regulated by the industry itself. Public access to decision-making and appeal is tightly constrained.

A corrupt institutional environment, then, and this is in lockstep with a toxic political culture, one in which hatred and payback are the *lingua franca* of public life. This percolates down, moreover. In his 2006 playscript, *The Bone Orchard*, Richard Bladel has a character, a 60-year old local forest campaigner, say this:

> We'd gone past some invisible point and it felt impossible to return. I wondered at the hate. The hate became incredible. You could feel it shivering off people. The town bitterly divided. Old friends no longer speaking. Old feuds and jealousies, long forgotten, reawakened with renewed venom. It was like some invisible plague had swept upon us, infected our minds overnight.

This is the front line – Tasmania's fractured forest communities – where forest politics really becomes vicious. And this is how the government wants it – because it believes that debilitating social conflict wins it elections.

We have, in these communities, a clash of values as strikingly divergent as can be found in all Australia. Over here are the people for whom the natural world is merely resource, there to be used as efficiently and on as large a scale as can be managed within the constraints of available technologies and stocks of raw material. And over here are those for whom the natural world is a source of transcendent meaning: the domain of spirit and wonder, a force and principle of life that enjoins respect, perhaps reverence. It is to live amid such transcendent natural values that the folk of the latter stamp have come to their chosen places.

You don't inherit place. You commit to it. You take its meanings upon yourself: its history, its rhythms, its defining character. When you make of a place a home – an affectionately regarded range of ground from which you take identity (literally your 'home ground') – you inherit an active duty of care. It is this sense of commitment that drives the campaign to protect Tasmania's remaining wild places. Unlike the Esk headwaters that have inspired these thoughts, not all of these places are forested. They include threatened remnant grasslands. They include Aboriginal coastscapes of incalculable human and natural heritage value, such as the midden, dune and scrub country of the Arthur-Pieman. In non-forest areas threats are more likely to emanate from resort and other brutalist building intrusions as money and influence ride roughshod over sound planning practice; from dune- and bush-trashing motorised off-road 'recreationalists'; or from the ignorant and bloody-minded racism that manifests in the wilful destruction of old-beyond-time Aboriginal artefacts.

It is time to say to government, you will not tear apart our home for a mere economic pittance. These wild temperate tracts exist nowhere else on earth, and in the complexity of living forms, processes and relationships that embody the island's soul are to be found values that cannot be comprehended within the price calculus of the marketplace. I say again: you will not lay the hand of death upon our home. We will – be assured – defend it.

'They Might As Well Cut My Brain Out'

(Originally a conference paper written for the 'Senses of Place' Conference in Hobart in 2006 ['"Balding Nevis": Reflections on an Unrecognised Constituency within Tasmania's Forest Communities and the Articulation of a Moral Economy of Place']. Versions of this essay have appeared in *Arena Magazine* in 2006 ['The Moral Economy of the Bush'], *Island* in 2010 ['"That Bush Up There Is All I Know": The Voice of the Voiceless in Tasmania's Forests'], and the *Journal of the Oral History Association of Australia*, also in 2010 ['"They Might As Well Cut My Brain Out": The Voice of the "Third Cohort" in Tasmania's Forests']. The *Island* and OHAA versions closely follow the text of a speech delivered at the Watermark Literary Dinner in Kendall, NSW, in 2009. A version of this paper also exists as an academic article published in *Geographical Studies* in 2008 ['"Balding Nevis": The Place Imperatives of an Invisible Cohort within Tasmania's Forest Communities']. The politics of Tasmania's forests have evolved since this paper was first drafted. I considered a substantial revision, but opted to let it stand. The text presented here most closely resembles the *Island* and OHAA versions.)

Can you recall the federal election of 2004 — the head-to-head between the now unlamented John Howard and the fatally erratic Mark Latham? Think back to October 6, the crucial final week of the federal election campaign, and the polls are all over the place. For reasons bizarre and wondrous, the detail of a so-called 'rescue package' for Tasmania's disputed forests has become the crucial election issue — the one that, it seems, is to determine the outcome of the entire election.

Each leader holds off, wanting to assess the reaction to the other's scheme before releasing the details of his own. It is classical electoral shadow-boxing, and the stakes cannot be higher. Latham's nerve breaks first — and his 'rescue package' is greeted with howls of outrage from the forest industry, including the Forestry Division of the CFMSU, an ALP affiliated union. The Prime Minister then announces his 'rescue package' for the forests. It is considerably less generous than Latham's in its industry restructure and compensation provisions, and it protects less of the forest estate, though not enormously so. But it is the politics that are all-important here, not the factual fine print, and Howard takes an extraordinary gamble — he announces his package at a Timber Communities Australia rally in Launceston.

And it works. A boisterous crowd welcomes him as lord and saviour, and vivid media imagery depicts a chuffed Prime Minister being slapped on the back by men jubilant and boisterous in singlets and flannel shirts. Leading the cheering for the Leader of the Liberal Party is Mr. Scott McLean, State Secretary of the Forestry Division of the CFMSU, a member of the Federal Executive of the Labor Party and subsequently an ALP candidate in the 2010 Tasmanian State elections — and not far behind Mr. McLean in the Vote-for-Howard-and-the-Liberals chorus is Tasmanian's very own ALP Government, and specifically its then Premier, Paul Lennon.

For most commentators this event was election-defining, and Labor lost two of its five Tasmanian House of Representatives seats — though it is noteworthy, I think, that opinion polls taken in the week before the rally had already foreshadowed large, seat-changing swings.

However — none of this is really to my purpose. What I do wish to observe is that, given the dramatic, highly visible nature of such an apparently election-pivotal event, it is probable that most Australians now see the timber communities as politically undifferentiated, with Timber Communities Australia unchallenged as their voicepiece.

On such a reading, conflict over the fate of the Tasmanian forests takes on a simple rural-urban configuration, the assumption being that opposition to forest practices is confined, in the main, to larger urban areas, with the position articulated by Timber Communities Australia — one of uncritical support for existing regimes and practices — *the* voice of the bush.

*

Though an entirely reasonable interpretation of the evidence supplied by the rally and the election outcome, such a reading cannot actually be sustained. The forest communities are anything but politically monolithic, and are, in fact, deeply conflicted. Most campaigns against contentious, coupe-specific logging proposals are initiated by *local* dissidents in the first instance, and even after the campaigns have gained momentum, and island-wide activist structures and personnel have swung into action, much of the energy and strategic savvy continues to be supplied by local people.

There is a tendency for local forest campaigns to be led by and largely consist of comparative newcomers to the communities in which they now live, and this is a political albatross of some significance. Their opponents in Timber Communities Australia, by contrast, make potent and ideological appeal to a generations-long continuity of involvement in the forest industries. And in 2006 the National Association of Forest Industries' Tasmanian director, Terry Edwards, claimed 30,000 members for Timber Communities Australia. But TCA has its own albatross. Its reputation in Tasmania took quite a hit in May 2006, when it conspicuously failed to defend harvesting contractors against a decision by Gunns Ltd. to cut long-term supply contracts in response to a sudden drop in woodchip demand, thereby inflaming a widely-held public perception that, far from being a grass-roots organisation created by and for the timber folk, TCA is merely a front for large industry interests, one that draws much of its funding and logistical support from the National Association of Forest Industries. I have myself interviewed an ex-staff member of Forestry Tasmania who claims that Timber Communities Australia was an initiative of Forestry Tasmania management – a claim that is sadly impossible to verify.

Many locally-focused anti-logging campaigners came to the communities in which they now live as long as 30 or more years ago, as 'alternative lifestylers'. Others are more recent arrivals, 'sea-changers' (sometimes unnecessarily re-labelled – by those apparently ignorant of the linguistical function of metaphor – 'tree-changers'). Usually articulate and educated, often refugees from professional stress in the large cities of mainland Australia, they bring much-needed capital and are frequently active in community re-vitalisation activities. In politics they are knowledgeable, confident, and strategic. The local landed and business elites who have always promoted economic development as a self-evident good, one beyond any need for reasoned argument, are now forced to compete with a resilient sub-culture of environmentalism.

Within Tasmania, at least, it *is* known that Timber Communities Australia is not the hegemonic voice of the bush, and the strong presence of alternative lifestylers and sea-changers within the forest communities is recognised. But this is not the end of it. A third group can be identified, one that shares the political aspirations of the sea-changers but has so little else in common with them that members of the two cohorts rarely make common cause.

The third group consists of people who, like the Timber Communities Australia constituency, can claim generations-long ties to the communities in which they live, including a continuous involvement in the forest industries, but who are staunchly *critical* of the harvesting regimes that currently pertain. They *tend* to be older people, but are not always so, and they are less visible because they keep their views largely to themselves. They do not join together in pursuit of common political goals, and they tend to avoid political structures set up by others, even when these are congruent with their own views and values.

It may be that in some timber communities they are such a small presence as to be almost negligible – though never, I think, entirely absent. But I have discovered one forest community where theirs is clearly the dominant voice. This is an upland community to the east of Launceston, a basin of land enclosed by the foothills of Mt. Barrow, Ben Lomond and Ben N*ee*vis (as the locals pronounce it), and its place is the catchment for Launceston's main domestic water supply, the upper reaches of the North Esk river.

It *is* just possible that this community is unique. A colleague who knows the southern timber town of Geeveston reports only small evidence of such a cohort there. On the other hand, in the Meander Valley, in the north of the island, it is easy enough to find people who fit the profile of the people I have called the timber towns' 'third cohort', though they are certainly not in the majority. As I investigate other parts of the island, though, I expect to find it a not inconsiderable factor within the demography of the timber communities.

In the North Esk country there are considerably fewer people than in the Meander, and the community infrastructure is restricted to one single community hall – no shop, school or church, not even a current graveyard. Yet this was once core sawmill country, with a network of self-contained villages attached to each mill. Most mills were small, but they included a couple – the Roses Tier mill, and Chesterman's mill at Burns Creek – that were among the largest on the island. Now there are only the diehards left, small sawmillers – not necessarily even old – retired millers, retired 'fallers' (as they call themselves), more men than women, and, as yet, no sea-changers.

In the place of which I speak a rapid conversion of native forest to plantation is occurring. It should be prime Timber Communities Australia country. It is not. 'Everyone around here thinks like me', said one outspoken sawmiller when I asked him how hazardous it was to excoriate forest practices in the way that he customarily does. And when I asked about Timber Communities

Australia he said, 'there's no Timber Communities Australia around here. They wouldn't get anyone to join'. Most have only the rudiments of formal education – sometimes not even that – but they are wonderfully articulate. They speak in a strong, old drawl, and they are brilliantly inventive in their deployment of language. 'They're baldin' er up there today mate', the same sawmiller said to me one day, waving at the nearby face of Ben Nevis. 'They're completely baldin' 'er'. 'Balding the mountain'. What a perfect evocation of the indignity visited upon the land by the contemptible practice of clear-felling!

The people of the upper North Esk hearken back to an economy based around small sawlog production for local or regional need. They carry a very strong sense of local history. They lionise the legendary bush-workers and communities that were here before them. They insist, furthermore, that such an economy remains viable, that the resource to sustain it still exists (though not likely to for much longer), and that it could provide sustenance for a network of small villages and towns, in place of the asset-stripping and depopulation that presently characterises the smaller centres within timber country. One sawmiller said to me:

> Even if they just save this little bit, and people get sawmilling going again, and everyone helping everyone out. People would say: 'gee, I'd like to live in that little town. Get businesses working again and farms going'. People want to stay, but what can they do?

The same sawmiller sees considerable irony in the 'Timber Communities Australia' sobriquet. Like many others, he sees the organisation as a front for a monopolistic industry that actually wants people *gone* from the bush. In interview he observed thus:

> they want to close the farms and the little towns down – they want a clear run at it out there, so they won't have to worry about poisoning people's water supplies, or

copping shit about the bloody arc lights that are on all night so they can just keep on working round the clock.

The anecdotal information I have is that most of the men working in the clearfells are *not* locals; many, indeed, are not even country people, but live in Launceston, Tasmania's second city, which is a mere 40 minutes distant, and which is, properly speaking, Tasmania's *largest* timber community, even though to live in the suburbs of Launceston is *not* to actually live in the bush.

Much of the antagonism towards current forest practices is directed towards its impact on water quality, particularly high up in the headwaters, where permanent hydrological changes are seen to be taking place. Some are scornful of industry and government scientists, who are thought to turn up to do their studies and take their measurements at precisely the times when they can be sure of *not* finding anything in breach of the Forest Practices Code. 'There are people up here can't read and write', said one local, 'and none of us are scientists, but we're here all the time, and we see things – dead wombats in the creeks and that, the creeks foamin' like y'wouldn't believe, algae up here where none's ever been known before – we see stuff that the bloody scientists never see because they aren't here when it's right there in front of you'.

Such an observation raises questions about the comparative status of grounded place knowledge versus the authority of science. Who should we believe? Scientists who turn up three of four times a year, stay for an hour, gather samples and take them away? Or local people of little or no formal education who have developed a keen eye for the most subtle of changes; who understand the land in its minutiae, and the nuances of its biophysical processes? The people of the 'third cohort' of the Upper North Esk know animals and animal behaviour, weather, trees – and they can also discourse idiomatically about soil types and properties, and about hydrological matters. And many are openly contemptuous of forest science as they have had experience of it.

On current 'falling' regimes there is similar scorn. 'We used to spend hours working out how to fall a tree so as to do the least damage to the forest', said one retired 'busher' – another local colloquialism – and then, with bitterness: 'I don't know why we bothered'. One of the sawmillers quoted above has a one-person mill that lies idle for most of the year. He insists that most of what goes to the chipper is 'millable', and that it is only greed, laziness and incompetence that condemns it to the chipper.

> I could make a year's living out of just one truck load going down the road there to St. Leonards – where they'll just say, 'no good, off to the chipper with it'. That's because they don't know how to mill. I do. I can get timber from logs that no-one else can. I could make a fortune out of the blackwood that's going to the chip. If they'd drop one log off here on the way I'd make more from that one log than they'd make from the rest of the load.

There is also much sadness for the animals and birds whose lives are destroyed in clearfell operations and the subsequent laying of 1080 poison. One sawmiller, a man who walks through the bush in all weathers in bare feet, who lives in a humpy at the centre of which is, I think, an old caravan, and whose home within fire-adapted bush is surrounded by old car bodies, spoke of the wild things of the bush in a way, and entirely unselfconsciously, that was almost primal. A recurring observation is that animals cannot live in the plantations, and that, along with the much publicised decline in the Tasmanian devil population – and the disease that is ravaging devil numbers was universally attributed to the chemical regimes deployed in forestry operations – the eastern quoll and tiger cat are also in significant decline, as are many species of birds. 'And there's a lot more roadkill now', one man observed to me. 'The animals are so docile with all that poison in them. Even the fish just lie there in the creek, with no energy'.

Finally, a tangible sadness hovers around the lives of these people. They are not optimists, and a sense of utter powerlessness overwhelms most of them. Stories are told of marriage and health breakdown – even suicides – as one social consequence of life within the devastation of the clearfells. That is one of the reasons why the gender imbalance is skewed. When families break up as a consequence of the stress of living in the midst of a devastated landscape, it is the women who move away. And when people die, widows move to town, and widowers stay put.

I struggled to comprehend the stress that these people are under. Remember that they are not politically confident or savvy people, and low or non-existent literacy levels prevail. Most are poor. Many simply cannot conceive of ever living anywhere else – or doing anything else. Then I heard a story that broke through that comprehension barrier. A sawmiller waved to the mountain at his back, and he said:

> That bush up there is all I know. I can take you up there and show you how the wind shifts when you go a yard or so that way, and how the temperature pools differently over there. And this summer they're going to flatten that bush. They'll plant it out in *nitens*, but it wouldn't matter if they let it grow back – it still wouldn't be the bush I know. And that's *all* I know. They might as well cut my brain out.

The scale and the brutalism of clearfell forestry ramifies throughout the island, with an unknowable but sizable proportion of all Tasmanians enduring deep and endless grief for the loss of the forests and the wild places. Richard Flanagan has written: 'not only the forest has been destroyed by this industry. Its poison has seeped into every aspect of Tasmanian life: jobs are threatened, careers destroyed, people driven to leave'. Observing that, 'after firebombing', a clearfell calls to mind images 'of the battlefields of great wars', he gives potent voice to the sadness and despair that are so prevalent: 'the great forests are gone, and they will not return, and nor will the intense human response we had to such places. Everything hereafter will be ordered and imaginable, paintable and representable in a way that those wild places never were, and we will be less'. If it is so for those of us who live many ridgelines distant from the devastation, imagine how much harder it must be for those who live, sleep and move about in its very midst.

I have no idea how prominent the voiceless 'third cohort' is within the wider mesh of forest communities in Tasmania – let alone the rest of Australia. It is an invisible community, its members lacking the political skills and confidence to organise or speak out, and for the most part they keep their views to themselves. It is not likely that they will be as prominent in most timber communities as they are in the one in which I have spent time, but neither are they likely to be negligible. Their existence greatly complicates present assumptions about the political complexion of the timber communities.

*

Let me, in closing, do a lap on one of my favourite hobbyhorses. The left of politics, where I have lodged all my adult life, dismisses the hearkening-back of my 'third cohort' as anti-progressive; as hopelessly romantic. Against this I would argue that whatever can defend collective vitality against abstract and frequently brutal market forces should properly be championed by people of progressive disposition. What, then, should be the response of the progressive wing of politics to the plight of the 'third cohort' of Tasmania's timber communities? As we have seen, these people hold a generations-forged sensibility of what is and what is not appropriate interaction with the ecological and social conditions upon which their way of life is based, a sensibility that is profoundly affronted by the practices and processes of present-day industrial logging. Can the values of these people really be categorised as a form of reactionary romanticism? For them change has brought with it a *loss* of individual and collective agency; a *diminution* of human potential. They are politically disarmed — but this only serves more dramatically to highlight the fact of disempowerment in the face of centrally-imposed economic structures, as well as the *anti*-progressive nature of technologically-rationalised change in forest practices and its incumbent human consequences.

The 'third cohort' within Tasmania's timber communities falls below the radar. It is of unknown numerical strength, not politically organised (and probably not amenable to organisation), and its likely survival into the future is tenuous at best. That it presently exists, though, challenges the predominant view that the bush is politically undifferentiated, a view that received considerable but tragically misleading affirmation through highly visible events during the 2004 federal election.

Going on 'The River'

(First published 1 July 2008 as 'I'm going on The River' in the souvenir program for the 25th Anniversary of the Franklin River Campaign.)

'I'm going on The River'. Someone says 'I'm going on The River' and there can be no doubting the river that is so signified. It is the river through which pours the pure, potent ichor of an island's thrumming heart – and, now, the river that distils an island's history, and its myths. The Franklin River.

The river holds all of time within its flow. I'd once thought Europe old – that I lived in a young place (post-invasion, anyway), one lacking any thread to a deep, unfolding past. All its history ahead of it. I'd thought this until I came to the Franklin, until the ancient Gondwana forests reached over me, gathered me into time itself, and my life changed, my scale of things, and my understandings of what is right and what is wrong.

I stand on a rock high above The Churn and there is a grip of fear upon me. I lose words. I lose personality – and this is disturbing and exhilarating, both. I am challenged to know myself; I am challenged to lose myself. Perspectives change. I travel an arc of time that has become no-time.

Long ages since, in caves downriver, the island's first people waited out the iron grip of the ice. It was here – somewhere here near The Churn – that Pearce the cannibal crossed. At Newland's Cascades Calder passed over with Lady Jane in her howdah, Sandy McKay dark and silent at her side. Against these cold, implacable currents ordinary supermen, Barnes Abel large among them, wrestled heavy piners' punts to attain the gold heart of the wonder wood, *Lagarostrobos franklinii*. Hawkins, Dean and co. are here. Bob Brown, resplendent in white Pelaco shirt, shoots Propsting Gorge. Men come with slide rules, theodolites and madness; and a brave and motley crew in rubber duckies comes too, to undo the insanity. The island's history and its politics is ever a contest about island meanings — those who see resource and money against those who see home and place, passionately loved simply for what it is, not for what it can yield. It is a contest that is ongoing, in which the Franklin River stands iconic.

*

The struggle to save the Franklin River was the first localised wilderness campaign to attain a planet-wide scope. The environment movement that it fine-honed — building upon the mobilisation of values and political strategy that began with the doomed resistance to the flooding of Lake Pedder — became, it could be argued, the most skilled and strategically astute environment movement in the world. And Tasmania developed a politics unlike any other in the world — a politics in which environmental issues, uniquely as I see it, sit permanently at the head of the political agenda.

The battle for the Franklin was won in large part because of the structures of Australian federalism, and the power of the Sydney and Melbourne media to transform the dispute into a national and ultimately an international issue. That is simply fact — and it is sobering to remember that the High Court decision that sealed the future of the great river (for the nonce) was attained by a single vote in a split decision. But to observe such and leave it at that is to do a profound injustice to those who went onto the river and into the forests — and thence to the island's courts — and whose very unyieldingness provided the bedrock in which more distant river-saving events lodged.

And it is to miss, too, the deep and lasting changes that the struggle for the Franklin wrought upon Tasmanian public life. For much of the twentieth century Tasmania's politics were moribund; a politics with no obvious values content; a politics in which the democratic skills ossified in the absence of discourse over dreams and principles; a politics entirely fixated upon administration; a godfather politics in which political disquisition joined sex and religion as topics unsuitable for polite dinner table discussion; a politics in which the democratic ground retreated to a small coterie of technocratic bureaucrats and Labor Party strongmen.

None of this was possible after the Franklin. The old anti-politics disappeared forever, consigned to history's dustbin by those who stood up and insisted that Tasmanians had not only a right but also a responsibility to confront issues of first principle. The fight for the Franklin gave birth to a democratic public sphere – a consequence as dramatic as it was unexpected. Many Tasmanians were uncomfortable with these new democratic realities, and godfather politics struggled churlishly on – most notably through the Premierships of Robin Gray and, yes, Jim Bacon and Paul Lennon. But after the fight for the Franklin the old don't-you-worry-about-that politics lost its clamp upon the civic culture. The democratic ground was been reclaimed by the people.

First principles, you ask? Oh yes. At issue was – and still is – the value to be accorded the quick skein of life that is the island.

Behind the chainsaws and bulldozers stood those who look at the complex, breathing livingness of the island and see mere resource to be pulled apart in the name of short-term economic imperatives. They are those for whom the Franklin is 'a brown, leech-ridden ditch' – and they are prominent in the Letters columns of the island's press to this day.

And in the rubber duckies, the Strahan camp and the city streets stood those for whom that quick skein of life contextualises humankind; provides telling counterpoint to the blind species arrogance that is drabbing down – perhaps destroying – the planet.

I'm pleased to nail my colours to the mast. The people I would want to make decisions on my behalf are those who have been to the Franklin, humbled people who see our place in the larger scheme of things, who have a sense of our species' strengths and weaknesses and a deep-commitment to the long-term — principled and large-hearted people who hear the speech of the river, and in the listening catch a hint of the island's soul.

*

How subtle the myriad shifts of tone in the Gondwana greens. The mauve tinge in the bloom of the mountain lilac. The cinnamon wash on the myrtle. The red splash of *blandfordia*. Intricate micro-worlds of honeydew, fern, small sedges. Imperious sea eagle. River-sheering tree martin. I wake in the morning to hear the river talk. I sense that it is a language I might one day learn.

Through the river slides a loop of memory. The people of kutikina are here. Snivelling, desperate Alexander Pearce is here. McKay. Goodwin. Abel. Hawkins. Dombrovskis. And James McQueen, who defiantly proclaimed the Franklin *Not Just A River*. Memories of the dead and of the living, and memories lodged in the inexorable processes of time that soar beyond the ken of humankind. Memories that slip along with the river, today, still — because the river, the island's great crucible of myth and meaning, flows yet, its heart pulsing free, its history brewed into a myth to sustain a people's self-regard.

It has escaped, for now, the fate that the heirs to the island's old inferiority complex had decreed for it. But there are yet those living among us who would reduce this marvellous island to the humiliating status of quarry; to just another featureless brick in the grey wall that increasingly hems the planet around. The River flows yet — but it was almost not so. It is time, then, to salute those whose collective determination and resolution saved the Franklin – and in so doing, preserved the rare and great in this wondrous island.

A Democrat's Lament

(This is a revised and much reduced version of a presentation entitled 'Democracy's Preconditions: Why They Are Not in Place', given at the Launceston Festival of Ideas, 2008.)

The British scientist, James Lovelock – described in the *New Scientist* as 'one of the great thinkers of our times' – tells us that, by the close of the century, the current population of Planet Earth will have been reduced by 80 percent. This will come about because our rapacity, our greed, our fetish with the raw level of economic throughput – growth – as the indicator by which we assess public wellbeing, will condemn us to destroy the life-sustaining integrity of our collective home. We have pushed the planet *past* the points of no return – what the literature calls the 'tipping points'. *Already.*

Very many scientists agree with this, though they don't say this in public. This is because of a view – misguided in my opinion – that to *not* offer hope to people and politicians is to deprive them of the necessary motivation to *strive*, politically, for change. They don't say this in public, then, but they most emphatically do so, many of them, in private. Tipping points having been reached, it is now too late to halt the melting of the Arctic ice. And this means, feedback loops being what they are, that it is now too late, as well, to halt the thaw of the heat-reflecting Greenland ice sheet. And as *this* cooling mechanism is lost, the rate of temperature rise will inexorably accelerate still further. CO^2 storing-algae that float on the surface of the oceans and are crucial to the production of rainclouds, will die. At a 4°C average planetary rise (on what already exists) the tropical rainforests – the lungs of the earth – 'melt away to be replaced by scrub and desert'. It is technically possible that such an event might bring on the collapse of the nitrogen cycle and the end of life on earth. Assuming this doesn't happen, we can anticipate a planet from which most oceanic life will have disappeared, and a baking, diminished land surface, whereon any mode of agriculture will not be possible. And for most of the globe, no water.

This is known. It has been known for two decades, even if the new, speeded-up timeframe over which this is happening has taken us by surprise. If you were to sit where I have sat, and had to deal with the avalanche of evidence that I confronted on a daily basis, you would know it, too – even the most sceptical of you. You would insist that dealing with the *consequences* that attend this issue – 'consequences' because it is already too late for *prevention* – must become the clear and overwhelming priority of democratic governments everywhere, and that this priority should brook no deflection, not even when assailed by dire economic circumstance.

So. How *have* democratic governments responded to this, the greatest challenge we have faced since the splitting of the atom – probably, indeed, the sternest challenge since the last great meteorite strike (back when democratic governments were, of course, nowhere in sight)?

They have simply not responded. To deny the reality of human-induced climate-change is now akin to maintaining a belief in a flat earth. Who, these days, is a flat-earther? Some rogue and irresponsible scientists prepared to take the devil's shilling are flat-earthers. Fanatical neo-cons in love with abstruse and arid abstractions of economic theory, and with no grip on the real world, are flat-earthers (unfortunately a self-perpetuating critical mass of them happen to be employed in the Murdoch media empire). And, of course, politicians are flat-earthers – very many politicians, here and elsewhere in the world's democracies, for whom Donald Trump, presumably the most powerful individual on the planet, can stand as paradigmatic. In my local rag a rare enlightened journalist, Peter Boyer, has just written of the 'political delusion' of leaders who construct themselves as climate change 'realists' — contra scientists and environmentalists, who are not. Such strange times we live in.

Through the 1990s we could have done something about the catastrophe that now impends — something *preventative*. Instead, the government of the most powerful nation on earth (and our national government, too, of course) was dominated by flat-earthers. And ten crucial years were lost.

*

Now, I'm not actually here to talk about climate change. What I want to ask is why it is that the world's democracies have proven so inept at dealing with an issue of such surpassing import and technical complexity.

We always talk about the wrong thing when we discuss democracy. We are doing it today. We equate democracy with the formal machinery of government, and we think that that is all there is to it. For a succession of US administrations on a mission to export 'democracy' to the non-western world it meant installing 'off the shelf' models of government wherein people get to periodically choose between an oil cartel billionaire and a defence contracts billionaire. This Wallmart-on-the-skirts-of-every-town notion of democracy — this anaemic concept of democracy as electoral contest between two blandly homogenised political organisations offering no greater order of choice than two rival soap powder brands on the supermarket shelf — this is a sham notion of democracy. Tinsel democracy.

There are very many definitions of democracy, and here's mine. Democracy exists when there is meaningful — as opposed to merely formal or symbolic — involvement of ordinary people in the shaping of the decisions to which they are thereafter subject.

And, democracy exists when the processes that *inform* their input to those decisions have integrity – are untrammelled and clear of obfuscation and manipulation. In the first instance, then, the test of democracy lies within civil society – the public realm – rather than the formal institutions of government.

Civil society has, however, abdicated its crucial role across much of its democratic range – I'll come back to this – and has vacated the field to formal structures, though these seem increasingly unable to deal with the difficult and complex problems of the times in which we live.

*

The problem of democratic structures is essentially one of mismatch between the increasingly *technical* nature of public decision-making, and the *amateur* standing of elected representatives. Legislators are teachers, farmers, company directors, lawyers – very many lawyers – often with highly particular professional expertise, and often with no particular expertise at all. They are, for the most part, spectacularly ill-equipped to make sense of the technical complexity that so much decision-making now requires. Almost none have professional training in a scientific discipline that seeks to explain how planetary systems work; how it all fits together. Climate change, then, is simply the most dramatic and dismaying example of a more general political pathology.

Now, it can be argued that this is actually *not* a problem – that the amateur has the capacity to render the technical and the complex simple, and to impose a commonsense perspective upon any apparently intractable or convoluted problem. My response to this is to quote the brilliant aphorism of H.L. Mencken and commend to you its good sense: 'for every complex problem there's a simple solution. And it's wrong.'

The evidence that this is how it is in the political system is abundant, perhaps most compellingly in the extent to which the decisions that so profoundly influence the conditions under which we live our lives are not made in the political arena at all. What *most* shapes our lives? Investments in new technologies. Do we debate, in the world's legislatures, whether to invest in this technology, or that technology? Almost never, and if we do, only at the edges. We may attempt to regulate the uses to which a technology is put *after* it becomes a reality, but mostly the first we know of a life-changing technology – the personal computer, say, or biotechnologies, or nanotechnologies, or even the good old internal combustion engine – is when they turn up, virtually unannounced, in our lives. One day they are just there, their costs and benefits not having undergone scrutiny or debate in any democratic forum – and our lives are changed forever.

Why has this happened? Because the very *complexity* of such decisions renders them not amenable to the democratic discourse, the latter being adapted to less technologically exuberant times – and so it is that this crucial tier of decision-making slips below the viewfield of democratic consideration.

Much of the problem stems from the progressivist ideology of industrial modernism, an ideology within which democracy is located front and square. The progressivist heritage has it that the world is on an eternal trajectory of positive change – *from* a given state to a better. Its key institutions are seen as 'can do' – as problem *solving*.

Formal democratic structures still function within that cocoon of myth. I think they are more problem causing than problem solving – and the crisis of democratic institutions, a crisis that the Brexit vote and Trump election have thrown into such sharp relief – stems from the disconnection between *institutional* faith in the myth of the 'can do' capacities of the structures of government, and the fact that large swathes of the population beyond those institutions no longer share the same faith.

The German theorist, Ulrich Beck, has written tellingly of the failure of institutions to respond effectually to the large-scale hazards that originally arrived, with the blessing of science, as problem solving. The disjunction lies in the risk-denying logic of contemporary institutions, which remain imprisoned within their nineteenth century problem-solving ideologies. Each hazard, as it manifests, is absorbed within a self-serving belief that 'lessons have been learned' and, therefore, the institutions of regulation and management are back in control. Beck has labelled this 'organised irresponsibility' – risk denial. But the people know – or at least they *feel* – that the risks are not under control. And so we get a crisis of trust – we no longer trust the regulators, we no longer trust the science, and we no longer trust the institutions of liberal democracy. These, having ceded all technical authority to technologists, have abnegated responsibility for the *most* important realm of decision-making – setting the priorities for scientific and technological research and the subsequent deployment of technologies in the real world.

We are left with what Beck calls a 'truncated democracy', one in which 'questions of technological change remain beyond the reach of political decision-making' – and one in which there is declining public faith.

*

Politicians respond to their own apprehension of irrelevance in several interconnected ways.

Defying the good sense of Mencken's aphorism, one of these ego-maintenance strategies is to strive to at least look (and, presumably, feel) like a leader. The pose one adopts is sure, emphatic, confident – an air of 'in command'. It is entirely fraudulent. Down with such false and dangerous 'leaders', say I. I want politicians to acknowledge the unbearable complexity of our times – and the impossibility of their effective management. I do not want politicians to say 'here I stand, and nothing will make me budge', but instead to confess to the difficulty of the policy struggle, and who will say something along the lines of: 'this is a complex and difficult problem, and I'm still grappling with the evidence, still trying to extract appropriate meanings from it, still weighing the many contrary arguments'. Or: 'last year I believed x to be the case, but in light of new evidence I now think y to be, on balance, the superior position'. For this to happen the media have to stop portraying open-mindedness, thoughtful consideration and tough-minded doubt as inconsistency, or 'flip-flopping'. I will never again vote for a politician who is unfailingly *consistent*; who never shifts as the evidence shifts for fear of appearing weak.

A second responsibility-avoidance stratagem is to retreat into science. Here science is seen to be monolithic (when in fact paradigms shift markedly from science to science) and certainly not to be interrogated. I've worked in the corridors of power and I've seen how all-pervasive the escape into science can be. A typical formulation might be: 'don't get emotional, you'll do your case no good – I'm only interested in what the science says'. The problem here is that much more of the work that the brain does is emotion-processing rather than reasoning. To react emotionally to any given circumstance is normal – and legitimate. It is the immediate mode of reaction when a judgement needs to be made – it is *everyone's* initial response, including those who claim to base their position on science or dispassionate reason. We are, in other words, primarily *emotional* beings.

A third such strategy, one increasingly prominent, is to do the exact opposite and declare science the problem. This is the ego-maintenance strategy of the rusted-on ideologues of the right, which is to crusade against a convenient scapegoat, to demonise someone or thing. And look now, here's science, the domain of the big-brained weirdos who made us feel stupid and inadequate in school. Perfect. Reject its very legitimacy then, especially where it would seem to undermine sacrosanct ideological precepts. If science and the tenets of your ideology are in conflict then science must have it wrong, for the articles of your faith are unshakeable, sacred, and beyond question. The apprehension of your irrelevance is screened out by the ideological fervour of your politico-religious belief. In the case of climate science this has resulted in the most spectacular and disastrous incidence of mass cognitive dissonance we have had to helplessly endure since the witch trials.

Finally, if one's electoral constituency is not particularly diverse, or contains a single dominant interest, the stratagem can be adopted of constituting one's role as a representative very literally indeed, and acting in public life as an unashamed agent for that dominant interest. I actually have a little sympathy for this position. I'm a 'strong democrat': in principle I agree that elected representatives should strive to be faithful to the views of those whose votes have placed them in a position of public trust. Indeed, in some circumstances it would be be an act of political suicide to act in any other fashion.

This would certainly be my stance in 'normal', which is to say, more placid, times. But the signature crises of the epoch – of democratic confidence, of faith in the problem-solving capacities of science, of the running down of the planet's vital life-support systems – give legitimacy to the position associated with the father of English conservatism, Edmund Burke. Burke argued for a 'without fear or favour' approach to the making of policy decisions; a stance of 'owing nought to any favoured person or group but only to the unmediated truth as the representative assesses it, having listened impartially to all shades of informed debate'. No relief here for the elected official, burdened with a sense of inadequacy, who would seek refuge in some reality-denying strategy of ego-maintenance.

*

But I've said that the true testing ground of democracy is to be found in the condition of *civil* society – the 'public realm'. Democracy demands an engaged and *activist* public realm. And we don't have it. The forums of public discourse are for the most part moribund.

Democracy does *not* exist simply when elected representatives act in accordance with public opinion. What matters is how public opinion is formed in the first place. If it is constructed via manipulated or incomplete information, or prejudice, or plausible-sounding cliché, it is not democratically legitimate. Democracy is, above all else, a *discursive* practice. The trouble is that, in these technologically complex times, the vector of technological change is essentially a privatising one – whilst the practice of democracy is inherently *social*.

That is why, as a democrat, I am not a liberal. Nevertheless, my guide and mentor in all this *is* a liberal, the great nineteenth century English liberal, John Stuart Mill, for whom active participation in the public realm was crucial for the practical, social and moral development of the individual. Such activity induces moral self-development in individuals because it serves the *public* interest rather than an exclusionary *self*-interest, and because one thereby learns to be other-regarding, unprejudicial, civil, fair, decent, and empathetic. Mill would have rejected the extreme form of liberalism which, for some inexplicable reason, we have come to call neo-*conservatism*, in which the basic unit of democratic life, the reasoning, discursive, amenable, autonomous citizen, morphs into the basic unit of the market, the impulse-driven, private, selfish, appetite-enslaved *consumer*.

*

I've come here with a problem. I don't pretend to have an answer – if I did I'd possibly be rich and famous, and that would never do. I think I know what is wrong, but I do not pretend to know how to put things to rights. I know that we lack certain essential preconditions for democracy. One is a vibrant public realm of citizen activity (in contrast to the hedonistic private realm of consumers that prevails). Another is a broad democratic competence and confidence in the assessment of scientific and technological futures – in contrast to the inept and bewildered legislatures that limp along in the face of technological and policy complexity.

Can these pathologies be fixed? I don't know – though I hope so. Is democracy intrinsically suited for the less complex times in which it evolved but no longer adequate for today's needs? It may be so – I hope not; would like to believe not. Is there hope? There's always hope, but I'm not the person to advise you where to look for it. I might not know how to bring it about, but I think I know what is needed. We need to take democratic control of technological change. And we need engaged, activist citizens, not mindless, market-cypher-reactive consumers.

I thank you.

Flow and Stasis on Tasmania's West Coast – The Emplaced Art of Raymond Arnold

(First published as 'Flow/Flux' in Raymond Arnold, Western Tasmanian Paintings, Devonport Regional Gallery, 2009.)

The first thing to be said about Tasmania's West Coast is that it is un-Australian.

Australia is 'created' in a certain way; it is dressed in a suit of ideas and images that configure it as a country, a landscape, a culture, a history unlike any other. Australia, we know, is a dry country baked to dust by an unforgiving sun, a 'land of sweeping plains' in which the eye roams to far, shimmering horizons. It takes its myths and meanings from this wide, dusty land. Its white-man history is wrought from the bringing of European agriculture to tired old soils, and failing often in unequal contests with the tyranny of vastness and the perennial absence of water. Lassiter. Burke & Wills. Goyder's Line. Names to sum a land, and a culture. Of course, the national imaginary is on the move. Stir into the mix the deeds of Australians in khaki upon battlefields 'far-flung'. And now, as the recipe globalises, add a large dose of beach and play and the new chic of the postmodern city.

But whichever way you twist it this is not the Tasmanian West Coast.

The place-forging geographic mark-points of the island's west are as remote from the signifiers of the national myth as they are from the moon. Water here is all-pervasive – it squelches underfoot, it slides coldly over boot-tops into sole and sock, it falls, it rises, it insinuates, is eternally restless. The water deficit that seems destined to engulf the planet may one day become a fact of life here, too, though possibly not to the same calamitous degree –

meanwhile, it is the *ubiquity* of water that configures the west. And as it is with the elements, so is it with the land. In place of endless plains of dust, scrub and sand and impossibly far horizons stand sharp-etched ridgelines of cold, enclosing mountains, their lower and middle slopes decked in a formidable spring of tangled growth.

This matters. Cold/hot, wet/dry, green/red, rock/sand, verticality/flatness — how the restless eye chooses from these stark dualities determines how place meanings are formed, mythologies created, vernacular technologies developed and deployed, and cultural expressions articulated. A prominent Australian poet once told me that Australian literature was sparse, dessicated and unadorned because that's how the land is. He was dealing in gross generalisation of course, and any number of writers can be adduced to point up the contrary, but I know what he meant. And the same might be said of the visual arts.

*

But now I have a question to set before you. It is this: what is to *become* of the West Coast? I do not primarily mean 'become of' in the portentous sense, though this is also important: more broadly, though, what is to be the fate of the West as a place in which people work and live and store memories, form attachments, and construct their place-specific personal identities? Its communities' futures have always been contingent on the continued abundance of the ore deposit, the fish, the power and the timber — and on the viability of market forces and technologies. But all ore seams are finite. Fish stocks experience ecological crash. Power generation technologies continually shift. Timber harvesting techniques and outputs blow with the political winds. Even tourist projections go awry as visitation fashions change. The West Coast has endured these catastrophic shifts to a greater degree than any other region within the island, and will probably go on doing so. It is a continuous work-in-progress with no guarantees, and indeed, the factors that will determine how the West 'becomes' are not, in the main, locally sourced. The only inevitability is that change *will* come. On the West Coast, all is flow.

All is flow. And this is so, too, even if we ignore the portentous connotation of that question: what is to *become* of the West Coast? Forests grow and die, species successions follow each other in the natural order of things, storms roll through, the climate shifts... all is flow.

*

Raymond Arnold knows this. He brings the extraordinary perspectival contrast of having lived and worked in the City of Light, the city of Manet and Monet, Degas and l'Autrec, Renoir and Cezanne, of the Revolution and the Commune, of Robespierre and Louise Michel, of the Moulin Rouge and Baron Haussman's boulevards, of Sartre and Camus. The Bayeux Tapestry and the battlefields of old and bloody Europe have commanded his creative intelligence – and this relatively recently.

And then, suddenly, he is living in Queenstown, on Tasmania's wild and remote West Coast, as far from the City of Light in real and spiritual terms as it is possible to be without leaving the planet. Yet Raymond has slipped deftly, unerringly, into the wild spirit of the West Coast. All is flow, and he recognises it so. He is drawn to the Iron Blow and the artistic results are memorable – but the Iron Blow is said to be critically unstable. Its state is one of becoming. At the Queen Valley mill the sawn logs, fussily geometric, are also in transformation to something else. Raymond sometimes depicts the mill and its stacked timbers from the other side of a wire-mesh fence, and the fence dramatically stoppers flow – not, I think, because the artist yearns for the futility of stasis, but to effect the pause that draws our attention to the very liquidity – the intrinsic transience – of the water-solvent wash that is the *becoming* of the West Coast.

Time, though, for a small complication. All flows – but it may be that not all changes. 'When I am painting', Raymond has written, 'my nose prickles at the Huon Pine perfume which is heavy on the air'. The West Coast flows, but within this flow there are constancies, certainties. Huon Pine, for one. Growth rings in venerable Huon Pine logs have been examined – in Canada, yet – for the light they can shed upon this old earth's changing climate. And on Mount Read a stand of genetically-identical Huon Pines, all naturally cloned (apparently) from a single male survivor of the last phase of glaciation, defies the human dynamism of today as it has defied the evolutionary hazards of its improbably lived ages.

Flux is the West Coast condition – but there are enduring marvels that anchor time within it. It is potent, passionate – a place entire unto itself. The fierce, creative intelligence of Raymond Arnold is at home here.

Politics and Primordial Time – Neil Hoffmann's Grand and Seamless Aesthetic

(First published in *Ceramics: Art and Perception*, No.29, 2009.)

Picture a cold, cold village hall in a small town in northern Tasmania. Those of us here in this wintry purgatory sit at trestle tables arranged in a horseshoe, and the mood is tense – because this is the Appeal Hearing into the controversial granting of a Private Timber Reserve at Reedy Marsh, not far from Deloraine.

'Reserve' is a weasel word – this is not a 'reserve' in the accepted sense of the term, but a concession to industrial forestry interests at the expense of community and natural values. And it is not easy to launch an appeal against a decision to approve a Private Timber Reserve in Tasmania. The legal window opens just the merest smidgeon. A Municipal Council has appeal rights, but the only permissible ground of appeal is a deliberately-kept-vague criterion called 'the public interest'. The Forest Practices Authority makes the call that any given timber PTR application is in accordance with the public interest, but how that determination has been made, and against what criteria, is never explained.

The Meander Valley Council has been inveigled into fronting an appeal on behalf of a group of Reedy Marsh residents, though the indications are that they now wish they hadn't. It so happens I know something about 'the public interest' and I'm here to give expert testimony on the appellants' behalf.

The residents run a brilliant case. They point out that the proponents have obfuscated the botanical character of the land in question, apparently to constrain awareness of the presence and standing of threatened floral and faunal species. They demonstrate that the planning status of forestry operations has been fudged to avoid the need to issue Permits. They demonstrate that the officer who drafted the PTR application subsequently had the job of assessing it. Those representing the proponents – Gunns Ltd. and a Government Business Enterprise, Private Forests Tasmania – are bored and tetchy. The man from Gunns, in cross-examination, asks me just two questions. How much was I paid to give evidence for the appellants? (Answer: not one red cent.) And, entirely ignoring all matters of substance in my evidence, he names instead a months-old date and asks: 'Did you address a rally organised by the Wilderness Society on that day?' That's it. The politics of smear – but just about as inept and pathetic a smear as you can possibly get.

And of *course* they are bored. I understand that. They know we are just going through the motions. They know the way the judicial winds will eventually blow. And so, despite the forensic force of the appellants' case, and the resentful perfunctoriness of the proponents', the tribunal finds against the appellants – as it was bound to do, given the political shockwaves that would be set in motion by a finding for the appellants. Such is the implacable way of forest politics in this gouged and bleeding island.

Next to me in the horseshoe is a man of quietly impressive demeanour, his hair pulled back in a pony tail. The sense is of intelligence, integrity and physical strength. This is Neil Hoffmann, Reedy Marsh resident and ceramist extraordinaire. He is very well met.

*

Months pass, and I am driving through Reedy Marsh in search of Neil Hoffmann's house and studio. Reedy Marsh is unlike the eucalypt forests I'm accustomed to down south. It is a distinctive sclerophyll forest on Aeolian dolerite in which *Eucalyptus ovata, pauciflora* and *viminalis* feature. It utterly enchants – but it is remnant; a *refugia* of a poorly reserved forest type that has been lost to land clearing across 95 percent of its original range.

I pass an old hut and come to a clearing, all that is left of a potato-grubber's bush run, abandoned these 80 years past. Here Neil has built two of his kilns. A little way down the track is a second clearing, and there is Neil's house and outbuildings, one of which is his studio-workshop.

The house, designed and built by Neil himself, is large, spacious, welcoming, and has a redolence of woodfire and good coffee. In the shrub that screens the large west window an eastern spinebill goes busily about its important work. Outside the house an old Fergie squats under the cover of an open shed. All is purposeful clutter.

The yard is enlivened with pieces, discreetly placed, from earlier phases of Neil's work. He talks me through these. First, his Dulverton Brickworks pieces from almost 20 years ago, when he moved playfully away from the potter's wheel and into figurative work. But the real sea change came with the 'Animate Earth' series that followed soon after with the construction of his first wood kiln. In this body of work the artist sought, through the medium of plastic clay, for earth-embodied suggestions of early life, and to extract this exploration from the intellect and its close collaboration with the hand, he engaged in 'unmeditated, random acts of making', working more remotely while shaping the clay, stretching it, throwing it around or 'working it blind' into a giving bed of foam, 'not quite knowing what would transpire'. The aim was to let the earth itself speak its piece; make its intent known, and the artist recast his own role more modestly – from that of god-creator to a medium through which elemental forces might conspire in the making of a truly grounded art; an art of the very earth.

Neil still likes these pieces, but came to the view that he remained too directing a factor in their making; 'too much a part of the work'. Seeking a working mode that still further privileged surprise and unplanned, organically-derived outcomes, he moved into larger, heavier pieces, 'pieces conceived in part by earth's gravity, as it pulled their wet mass deep into a bed of thick foam', before returning again to smaller works in which the play of opposing forces is the thing, seeking an artist's communion with the deep geophysical past, 'to cut back in time to earlier and yet earlier notional life'.

Outside again, we track back to the clearing up the road and the broader of Neil's Bourry kilns. 'It's a good kiln', he tells me, 'and it suits what I'm doing at the moment'. But this is an artist of ideas and a driving central vision, not a technocrat. He has no obsession with the detail of the kiln's chemistry; rather, 'the process is a catalyst for my thinking about larger issues'. The firing is a time of portent, of possibility, of wonder: it involves 'taking on elemental forces, and from the play between them, reaching toward an older world, and reflecting on our place in it now'.

Readers of *Ceramics: Art and Perception* will know some of this, for Neil Hoffmann has been featured here before. What has not previously been discussed, though, is the deeply political context to his work, and the extraordinary cosmological range of his aesthetic. That is why I have dwelt at such length on the political threat that local forest operations pose to the place and ecosystemic integrity of the artist's home range. And it is why, in tracing the evolution of his art practice, I have sought to explicate its links to the sweeping ambition of his aesthetic. Let me expound upon this for a moment, for it will not be immediately obvious how the reach into deep time of the artist's aesthetic links to a politics of the here and now.

Hoffmann partly entitles a sustained meditation upon his own creative project 'Imagining Genesis'. It is a visual meditation with text and it is quite remarkable. There have been creative and philosophical sensibilities before Hoffmann's that have scoped their dreams and their speculations cosmologically. But Hoffmann is different. Whereas other cosmologists swirl away into astral infinity, Hoffmann remains on – or in – this earth. He, too, swirls away – but he spins down through the flux and stream of deep time, down, down to the earth's first primal moments. He puts it better himself than I ever could: he seeks 'expressions of earth's first rumblings for life, of... a time before the substances within the earth found mobility, pre separation [of life from its source], pre independence'. There, in the energies born of the primordial moment, is to be found the essence – the *truth* – of all that the vast forces of time itself have bequeathed to us here, now. And that includes – especially includes – life on earth.

*

How does the grand sweep of this aesthetic shape, in turn, the man and the artist? It does so in three potent ways (possibly more – but these are three that I identify).

First, and most obviously, there is the impact of this fierce attunement with the unfolding process of geophysical time upon Hoffmann's art practice. In previous discussions of the latter much has been made of the meaning that Hoffmann derives from his medium/material – clay – and from the creative technologies of his wood-fired kilns. I have followed suit, and Hoffmann, too, has contributed to these ruminations. In an ultimately unused artist's statement for the 2005 Australian Woodfire Survey Exhibition in Canberra, he wrote:

I'm pushing clay and fire to speak their secrets, their knowledge of a time long past when life was in its most elementary state. I'm seeking to discover something of the primal energy, spirit and potency of the subterranean... I deliberately call in the power of the elements to take their effect on the materials I place in their path in order to imbue my work with manifestations of nature – the results of colliding forces and elemental friction. In this way I'm able to ride with nature for a while and feel something of its power.

Similarly, in the firing Hoffmann sometimes seeks to 'apply melt to the whole form, not just the surface, as is most common in ceramic practice'. In his mind, he says, is engagement with 'the earth's molten core', and he seeks the volatility of process and effect that is there in the earth's liquid heart; a 'greater relinquishment of control'. To American ceramist, Jeff Oestreich, Hoffmann's forms 'seem as if they are born rather than made... untouched by human hand'. I agree. It has already been noted that the artist seems less a creator than an enabler – a medium through whom the very earth speaks.

More recently, though, following the relentless pull of his deep-time aesthetic, Neil has moved beyond clay to an even more primordial substance – the bones of the earth: rock. In his series of clay melts Neil used clay taken from his own property. 'Giving the mother material life' was his evocative description of the project. But the primal vortex of deep time continued to beckon, and it was, he says, 'a logical extension to take the local dolerite and melt that directly'. 'If clay is mother', he has written, 'then rock is GRAND mother!', with 'earlier stories to tell regarding a geo-primordial time which notionally gave rise to our being'.

Hoffmann is much taken with geologist David Leaman's description of the local dolerite as 'The Rock Which Makes

Tasmania'. And so we come to the second important way in which his aesthetic constructs a lived unity of artist and man. The primordial processes of deep time emerge into the *here* of the artist's time and place, which happens to be the island Tasmania, and within that, the dolerite-birthed forests of Reedy Marsh.

The geophysical scapes and processes within which we move – along with our co-evolutionary travellers on life's grand adventure – embody the *memory* of all that has gone before and that has shaped our present. It links us to those evolutionary travellers who have stepped out of time, 'creatures which now reside only in the memory of the earth'. The artist describes this connection as 'umbilical', and it leads us to a 'heritage of connectivity' that joins us in space as well as time, so that a profound empathy for 'all tenants of this earth' ensues. This is rendered personal and immediate when it comes to the living forms (and the processes that sustain them) within the direct range of our own lived experience. It leads Hoffmann himself to a passionate concern – artistic and human – for 'the architecture of our place, our home', and the project becomes, then, one of place- or home-making: 'the establishment of an environment for birth, a place in which to dwell'. From a cosmological aesthetic that carries the artist down to the very moment of the earth's genesis, then, emerges a deep, seamlessly-derived commitment to localised place in the present.

You can see where this is going. You can see what this means for the artist's *apparently* non-political aesthetic. The third component of the artist's aesthetic trinity, then, is the political critique it engenders.

It is, he writes, 'time to grow our imagination and energy for restorative action'. It is time 'to change the collective consciousness for a new sort of doing'. It is time to 'naturalise' human behaviour so that we can rejoin the 'dance with our parent earth', 'regrow our visceral consciousness'. But on Hoffmann's island home a venomous marriage has been enacted between the suits of politics and the suits of capital to invest in life- and place-contemptuous resource-extraction. This is a loveless marriage, one with no feeling for that wild dance that is the island's bequest from the grand processes of deep, unfolding time. It is entirely appropriate that the artist should write: 'the greatest strength in what I make is not of my making'. It is entirely appropriate, too, that the artist should take his place behind the trestles at those sour proceedings in that grim and cold country town hall. Because the place, the man and the artist inhabit a single, continuous plane – a unity that joins a primordial earth-aesthetic to local, place-defending activism.

The Gallopers: 'Time Gone By Is Here Today'

(First published in *Forty Degrees South 47,* in 2007, and subsequently revised several times, though not again published.)

Prominent within the rotating circus of island festivity was, until very recently, an old steam-driven carousel. 'The Gallopers'. It had become such a feature of the 'festscape' that we assumed it an integral and essential part of our island's infrastructure of fun.

But we should not have assumed such inevitability. 'The Gallopers' was a wondrous artefact fetched up here on these shores, and the last thing we should have done is take it for granted. For it is no longer here. It has been whisked away, in the face of state and local government indifference.

It was the much-loved adoptee of Mark Money and his ex-bank manager wife, Judi, who happens to be my sister. In search of a long-harboured dream, Mark answered an advertisement in a British trade paper, travelled to Europe, looked down upon a disassembled 'pile of stuff', packed it in a shipping container, and brought it to Tasmania.

Even then it was rare and valued – 'but it was wrecked'. It wasn't until Mark tried to fit piece with piece that he discovered what he had and what was missing. The carousel had been taken from an English beachside amusement park to storage in Holland, where it was systematically plundered for parts, with many of the original horses and cutglass fittings sold off as collectibles. Mark set about replacing the missing parts, fashioning many of them himself, including missing components of the steam mechanism. It was a five-year labour of love.

Tasmania's steam carousel was one of a mere handful in all Australia, and undoubtedly the most remarkable – the largest, the oldest, and the most imaginatively presented. 'THE WORLD'S FINEST OLD GALLOPING HORSE RIDE BUILT 1885 FOR YOUR PLEASURE AND ENJOYMENT. YOUNG OLD. TIMID BOLD. TIME GONE BY IS HERE TODAY', proclaimed the message on the top curtain, and I am not going to argue that it wasn't so.

The carousel is powered by a two-cylinder steam engine which drives a large gear wheel connected by a central shaft to the 'spinning top' ('is powered'? I'm not sure what tense I should be using here). A large circular gear is bolted to the top of the shaft, and this engages toothed gears (dolly wheels) that drive the horse crankshafts in a lifting and dipping motion – a technology actually patented only a few years before its installation in 'The Gallopers'. (I could follow Mark that far – but it gets pretty complex: dolly wheels, quarterings, putlocks, pinwheels, cheese wheels...) Even now it's all too improbable for some. 'You'd be amazed how many Doubting Thomases drift by', says Mark. 'Blokes who insist it's really electric – one chap even looked me in the eye and told me the fire was a fake'. He tells it lightly, but it's plain that it rankles, too.

And then there's the organ that always travels with the roundabout. Traditionally the organ sits in the middle, but Mark has it set up to the side, so that his gateman/woman can leave the gate if need be, fine tune the organ, and be right back on the gate. For many years the gateman was an Anglican clergyman, Robert, who was also a dab hand with the mechanics of the organ: 'he was a diamond', says Mark, 'in the early days I'd have been lost without him'.

The organ is a mechanical wonderland in itself. Its music is generated by 'notesticks' – perforated cardboard that passes over a key frame, where a metal peg probes the perforations to 'read' the music – 150 tunes in all. It's a delicate mechanism. The smallest piece of fluff can jam it, whereupon 'Daisy, Daisy' dissolves into the most awful cacophony. Not that this happens very often – a bigger irksomeness, says Judi, is that 'weeks later you'll be going about your business, driving along perhaps, and "Daisy, Daisy" will still be playing over and over and over through your head!'

Though it is not an integral part of the mechanism, Mark insists that the organ is quite central to the experience: 'it is the draw – the magnet that draws you in. It provides that essential old-world atmosphere'. Not that the ride is exactly sedate. It drives quite quickly, certainly faster than many expect. 'It is a much more *thrilling* ride than the other Australian carousels offer', says Mark – for this reason everyone on the ride, adults too, must be seated.

There are those for whom the charm of 'The Gallopers' is irresistible. 'Some children get so attached to a particular horse – "Alice", say – that they will only ride that horse, and once aboard they might stay on it for up to six hours.' What about adults? Women, certainly, though men traditionally take more prodding. 'Dads ride', says Judi. 'It's the young men who think it's not cool'. Except on New Year's Eve, when 'you learn to expect the unexpected – and if there's ever going to be a spot of drink trouble, and there rarely is, that's when it will be'.

*

I have written my account in the present tense, because that's how I think of it and would like to go on thinking of it. But Mark's health declined, and assembly and dismantling are physically arduous. Then there's the tricky economics. The carousel took two long days to put together, and as much to take apart. It required a wages equivalent of $1300 for each process, and finding that labour became increasingly difficult. These diseconomies meany that little country shows were only feasible on the rare occasions when show organisers consented to underwrite the costs, or arrange some form of sponsorship. Thus it was that 'The Gallopers' eventually became a fixture only at 'The Taste', Wynyard's Tulip Festival and the Deloraine Craft Fair, less regularly at the Launceston Show, with other occasional one-offs.

Then Mark's health took a serious nose-dive. The carousel sat idle, was put on the market, and was eventually bought by a Victorian farmer, fated to sit in a paddock. So it was that marvel of the nineteenth century fairground was lost to the island. 'People here talk about "our carousel" now', Mark said to me. He would have liked the people of Tasmania to own it in Trust. For that it needed a permanent base – and a great deal more official interest than was forthcoming. Mark mused ruefully on the Geelong waterfront's much inferior *publically funded* steam carousel that is housed in a purpose-built (by the state) multi-million dollar seafront building. Canberra and Sydney, too, have state-owned carousels lodged upon permanent sites.

But Tasmanian officialdom remained maddeningly apathetic. 'The Gallopers' fell through the cracks – not Aboriginal heritage, not natural heritage, not lodged within our own early industrial heritage. But it was a colourful and joyous part of our recreational history. We have such a rigid view of what, from the past, merits protection. Grand colonial piles, but not the rustic timber sheds in which the work of old was done, not the machines with which it was done – and not the infrastructure of pleasure to which people turned to escape from the weariness of work. If I had the power I'd consign such heritage inflexibilities as are embodied in, say, the Burra Charter, to the scrap heap. What we call 'heritage' should never be reduced to an inflexible set of precepts or standards of almost mathematical exactitude, and devoid of particular context. And, most emphatically yes, I'd have 'The Gallopers' in public hands, and working the festivals of the island that, for too short a time, deemed it a key part of the complex that makes our home.

*

I once asked Mark whether he would he do it all again? His response was unequivocal. 'Absolutely! The day it first operated and I saw the joy on people's faces, I knew I'd done a worthwhile thing. I never think of the value of it – but it's something that isn't from this span of life, and that's a large part of its mystery.'

Ah yes. And I, too, loved the old carousel. The grace in the dip and soar of the horses. 'Daisy, Daisy'. And the banners depending from the spinning top, passing over me and out of view. There goes Malcolm Fraser, Paul Keating, Hawke, Menzies, Stalin, old King George, Harold Wilson, Einstein, Churchill, Florence Nightingale – was it? – and is that Garibalidi? 'Everyone is happy on the roundabout', Mark once said to me. 'When I see all those people smiling I think, oh, this is wonderful! That's why I do it'.

Or, to get the tense right, that's why he did it.

Ghosts of the Jungle

(Not previously published, and written some years after the events it describes. I have diary entries that cover this time, but I was unable to find them. It's possible, then, that some of the detail here reported may be in error.)

In 2012 I attended the Anzac Day service at Hellfire Pass on the Burma Railway. It was a memorable day, and I'll tell you about it shortly ('shortly' in both senses of the word), but this essay is really about the foolish escapade I undertook on Anzac Day eve, in the jungle of the Sai Yok National Park, up the line from Hellfire Pass.

I have a second cousin, a generation younger than myself, who runs a martial arts gym (and a travel agency) in Victoria. He is a wonderful man, and I wish I saw more of him. Every year he takes a party of martial arts adepts to Thailand for instruction and, for some, competition in Mai Tai, better known here as kick boxing. In 2012, out of the blue, he contacted me to ask whether I'd like to come along. I didn't even have to think about it.

*

We are a mixed crew, our ages spanning the teens to the high 60s, with 'our' martial arts interests running the entire gamut from a spiritual devotion to Tai Chi, through to the crunching physicality of Mai Tai. Those at the latter end of the spectrum – the majority – tend to be hard men, some of them earning a living in security for nightclubs, some as bodyguards for shadowy figures from society's underbelly. My cousin – let's call him Matt – gathers these men together as they fly into Bangkok Airport from different directions, installs us – as you see, I've now put myself in the frame; I hope that's not too much of a liberty – installs us in a noisy, somewhat decrepit bus, and off we clatter, sounding not unlike a herd of superheated 2-stroke lawnmowers

We stop first at Kanchanaburi, the Allied war cemetery, and the famous Bridge on the River Kwae Yai.

Why does Matt do this? Because he wants these hard men to know of the harder men of a generation prior, men who endured unspeakable torture and random brutality. He wants to instil in his charges a civic pride, one based not on the cheap slogans of the Cronulla race riots, but knowledge that is only to be gained through an on-ground familiarisation with those awful mid-century events that took place right here. When I first meet these men, I am more than a little intimidated. They ooze aggression – and they are big and fit. It doesn't help that they regard me with puzzlement, not knowing where I fit. But I needn't have been concerned. They defer to Matt in everything. Without any muscular show of authority, he marshals his crew with a confident aplomb. His very presence commands respect, and he is accorded it.

We swing west from Kanchanaburi, eventually passing the access road to Hellfire Pass and its deservedly famous museum, before turning left into Sai Yok National Park and crossing the embankment of a decommissioned railway which, I realise, has to be the Burma Railway, before stopping in an open space above a large river, the Kwae Noi. We have barely sorted our gear when cousin Matt, without warning, puts me right on the spot – and resolves, for the martial arts folk, the mystery of my presence on this trip. I am here, he tells them, because my father had been a prisoner-of-war forced to work on the Death Railway, and I will now tell them about it. There is a moment of panic – and then, recovering as best I can, I do just that. I speak of my father's capture in Timor, where, as Warrant Officer Reg Hay TX3713, 2/40th Battalion, he gathered together the cooks and clerks from Headquarters Company, told them to fix bayonets, and led them in a charge uphill and across open ground, to dislodge a Japanese machine gun nest that had a substantial section of the battalion pinned down, an act for which he was subsequently awarded the Military Medal. I tell them of his experience on the Death Railway where, not all that far from where we then were, he would stand between a brutal Korean guard and his work party to cop the bashing routinely handed out by the man nicknamed the Black Prince. I tell them of the day-by-day heroism of the NCOs, the men who became de facto officers, the 'real' officers having been separated from the 'other ranks' and quarantined from daily involvement in the utter awfulness involved in building the railway.

I must have talked for some time, because I spoke of much more besides. I know I talked through a silence I had difficulty interpreting, and I should remember what happens when I finish, but I don't. There may have been applause. I know Matt speaks briefly, movingly. Then we descend to the river and a small aquatic village. Here we stutter along a series of rickety, swaying footways before encamping in a stylish, substantial houseboat. This was the day before the day before Anzac Day.

In the late afternoon we board a second, smaller craft, a barge of sorts, and cast off, to drift along the bank to a gentle fall of water steepling into the river. Here, having moored against a rudimentary handlock, my fellow Mai Tai devotees strip buck-naked to cavort under the plash of the cataract. I do not. I am standing apart from it, and am, I think, the first to notice another houseboat drifting towards us. Not quietly – there is a deal of riotous joy coming from this houseboat which, as it draws nearer, can be seen to contain a cargo of white-fleshed nudity, and young, blonde, female nudity at that. It is also clear that its destination is the same thread of waterfall beneath which we are moored.

There being only one mooring point, this drifting raft of nubility has no option but to grapple longside us, and suddenly our houseboat is a-squirm with Australian martial arts aficionados and beautiful young Russian (as they turn out to be) escapees from a Norman Lindsay bacchanalia. Matt sternly forbids any touching, and he is, of course, obeyed without demur. There's a lot of Russian money in Thailand, and most of it is in the sex trade, so I hope I'm not doing the young women a disservice when I surmise that these are high-end prostitutes. Anyway, they turn my hard-as-nails shipmates into foolishly-grinning innocents. It is a joy to behold.

Eventually the sea of bouncy white flesh washes back onto its own houseboat, a motor starts, and the spirited young women move away against the current to wherever it is they have come from. We, too, start our motor and proceed slowly upstream to our mooring at the small floating village. I scour the steep bank for any sign of animal life, but see none. We moor and are sumptuously provided for. It is marvellous, but it sets me a little out of sorts. What would my father, just a small distance back in the jungle and starving, have given for food like this?

*

The day before Anzac Day. A day of leisure. Everyone wants to spend it cavorting under the fall of water downstream. I tell Matt I'd rather stay on the houseboat for a quiet day reading. The truth is, I'm hatching a plan, and it involves disobeying Matt. 'Do not walk off into the jungle by yourself', he has instructed us, and he expects to be obeyed. But his soft, bookish, unfit cousin is not to be trusted. We are in the Sai Yok National Park. During the night the penny has dropped. The sector of the line on which my father was deployed was administered from Kinsaiyok. Sai Yok. Kinsaiyok. Right here! Up the bank and through a narrow strip of jungle is the Death Railway exactly where my father spent the worst days of his life. The downstream-drifting barge is barely out of sight when I am away, crossing the rickety walkways, up the steep bank, and into the jungle. The walking is easy. This tropical jungle is not like the thick, tangled temperate stuff I know from back home. Walk away from the river, I tell myself, and you will soon come to the Railway. And I do.

I hit it a mere hundred metres from the road crossing on which we entered the park. Between these two points there is a building. I was vaguely aware of it when we drove in. It turns out to be the old Kinsaiyok Railway Station, still standing. The jungle is clear around it, and it is obviously maintained. Not only that, but it is maintained in part as a shrine to the Railway dead – and maintained, it would seem, by local people – or, at least, maintained unofficially. The slightly quirky use of English gives this away. It's going to be an emotional day. It already is.

My father would have worked both up and down the line from here, but I'm going down – because seven ks down towards Hintok was Jungle Camp No 1, where my father endured the brutalities of the infamous Black Prince. In Peter Henning's *Doomed Battalion*, at p276, I read:

> ... the Australians were split into two sections, one group with Reg Hay in charge working back towards Hintock under the supervision of the irrationally brutal 'Black Prince', the other with Ian Boreham under 'older Nips, civilian engineers under military control, but more considerate to work for'. Boreham and Hay tried to arrange for the groups to be rotated on a regular basis so that one group was not consistently exposed to the treatment of the 'Black Prince', but were not successful.

Jungle Camp No 1. I am going to find it.

The going is easy. I am on a railway embankment, after all, and it is gently downhill. I wish I knew the names of the trees. A little further down the line, from the Hintok Road crossing, past the site of the Three-tier Bridge, through Hammer & Tap Cutting and on into Hellfire Pass, the forest has mostly been cleared, with only bamboo remaining. Tom Uren lived and worked on this sector of the line. On his first trip back Tom was struck by, and lamented, the absence of the forest. It is this sector of the line that is best known. But the next sector up-line, that on which my father worked, is in the National Park, and here the structure of the jungle remains largely intact. It is, then, substantially as it would have been when my father slaved here.

I grew up hating the Japanese. We children of the line, most of us, did. I have twice been to Japan, and there I searched for contemporary manifestations of the rampant militarism of the 1930s and 40s. In vain. The accepted line is that the war's end saw a comprehensive destruction of Japan's imperial ambitions along with the culture that went with it, but that seems to me a little too glib. The fiercely militaristic culture is still there, I know, but you have to look hard and long to find it. I did look hard and long, but I didn't find it. I found, instead, a gentle, pleasant and thoughtful people. It was impossible to trace a line from these people back to the violence of the Railway. Many years earlier I had given voice to this confusion in letters written to Tom Uren and Arch Flanagan, wise and deeply compassionate men who I have long admired – and who were members of Weary Dunlop's 'Thousand' on the Railway. I asked each of them how they had returned from the Railway with a profound sense of humanity not only intact, but enlarged. I cannot, just now, put my hand to Tom's letter, but here I have Arch's, written in black ink, in a beautiful semi-cursive hand.

In his tribute to Tom Uren, *The Fight* (written in 2004), Martin Flanagan writes: 'They hated, those men who suffered on the line. Some hated to the grave, some await death with hate in their hearts. Weary hated. He told me that.' And Arch, too, expresses ambivalence towards 'the Japs', as he still (this was also 2004) called them. He recounts the story of the bashing and death of his good friend, Mickey Hallam, an event that has had a profound effect on him, and which has, in turn, figured large in the sensibilities of the Flanagan children. Martin and Richard have both written of it. In his letter Arch writes: 'I could forgive those who made life hard and unpleasant for all us others, your dad and me, were it not for the fact that in doing so, I would be deserting those who died in the camps hungry, dirty and homesick, hating the Japs who had brought them to this pitiful end'. But 'we must forever live in this indefinite world, keep the dislike within us dormant and let the like grow and flourish, for only thus can we develop as human beings'. Weary Dunlop, 'the great one', forgave them, Arch notes, and so did Tom Uren, because 'no man can live on hatred'. Arch himself, not long after penning his letter to me, was visited by three Japanese women who, deeply shamed by the atrocities carried out by their military during the war, wished to express contrition. I know this gesture affected Arch profoundly. In some ways I wish I'd written my letter subsequent to this.

This ambivalence is much in my mind as I set out to walk down the Railway in search of Jungle Camp No. 1. I can feel its corrosive power – the ambivalence I mean. It eats away at the pillars upon which I have constructed a capacity, I hope, for an other-regarding compassion. My very humanity seems under siege. It is not, I realise, as firmly founded as I would like, and for this I feel diminished. Those who suffered directly have good reason to hate. For such as me, a generation on, it is more morally complex. Of course, I did not have Arch's letter with me, nor the books from which I have quoted, but the same inchoate swirl of emotions that accompanies the writing of these paragraphs was with me then. So – I walk.

Nothing moves in the jungle. The heat builds. Beside the embankment are occasional deep cups in the ground. Craters of American bombs, I wonder? There is no other obvious human element, the embankment of the line excepted. I begin to find this strangely unsettling. I walk on.

Martin Flanagan calls Ray Parkin 'the great writer of the Burma Railway'. Parkin wrote a trilogy of Burma Railway books, not much read now, and to my shame I have to admit to not having read them myself. But 'in addition to recording what went on in the camps', Parkin, writes Flanagan, 'was absorbed by what went on around them, the plant and animal life, the climate and natural terrain'. I envy him. The jungle is so alien. I wish I could name the species. I would, I am sure, feel much less discomforted. I walk on.

Everywhere water flows. The culverts have been washed away, and I must wade through small, shin-deep streams. I recall reading somewhere that the diseases with which the prisoners were afflicted were mostly water-borne. My own growing dis-ease ratchets up. Then, too, somewhere ahead of me is Hintok, where the men camped in 'Tiger Valley', and where 'tiger fires' were lit at night to discourage these, the most magnificent of predators. As far as I remember there were no deaths by tiger during the construction of the Railway, but it is technically possible that the jungle through which I am walking still contains some. I wish, now, that I had obeyed my cousin. But I walk on.

Not all that many years ago a recovery party worked the line to find the last few previously unlocated trackside graves in order to have their occupants repatriated to the Kanchanaburi War Cemetery. One of the few graves located was at Jungle Camp No 1, and, as I remember, was that of a $2/40^{th}$ man. The jungle camp was a primitive affair. It is impossible that any infrastructure remains – the jungle will have reclaimed it. I'll not recognize it. I'll walk straight past.

I have no idea why, but still I walk.

I am struck again by the realisation that the jungle here today is little different from the jungle my father knew. And now an appalling thought occurs. Up ahead is a clump of bamboo. I stop.

I stare at it – and I expect to see a skeletal man with a drum-tight covering of skin, weighing nothing, and clad only in a tattered loincloth, step from behind the bamboo. *And if that man is my father, he'll be the kid, and I'll be the old man.*

The thought cannot be borne. I turn on my tracks, and don't stop until I'm alone on the houseboat, pretending to read a book.

*

The next day is Anzac Day. We reach Hellfire Pass in the pre-dawn dark, gather with others in a large and quiet throng, candles pricking the dark. As ever, I remember few details of the service. It's the atmosphere that's the thing. It's why I go, back home, to the late morning Anzac Day service. The dawn service is too religious and I'm an atheist, so I stay away from that one. The later service is more secular, and it has the march. When there were still 2/40th men marching behind the Battalion's flag I would be kerbside in Macquarie Street, teared up. These days it's the service that renders me an emotional wreck, particularly those mournful hymns, 'O God Our Help in Ages Past' and Kipling's 'Recessional'. I know this is high British jingoism, but what matters to me is the pure essence of grief that they embody. I soak it up, mourning the father who died suddenly when I was 13, and more recently, mourning, too, my lost son, who had become a companion on the Anzac Day marches. But I have written about these matters elsewhere, in 'The Silent Fathers' to be precise (my best piece of prose), so I shouldn't reprise such old and trodden ground here. I should just note that today, here at Hellfire Pass, is a memorable day. I have attended a dawn service again, in an extraordinary, ghost-haunted place, and it is forever etched in my mind.

The service ends in daylight. Hellfire Pass really consists of a series of cuttings, the most dramatic of which is Konyu, and that is where we are now. Sheer walls of hard black rock, hand-hewn by an army of starved and disease-ridden men. It is scarcely believable. Then, too, in our xenophobic way we tend to lose sight of the fact that by far the bulk of the workforce consisted of press-ganged Asian labourers, with Tamils, Malays and Burmese prominent among them. Of the 270,000 in this category, as many as 90,000 died. Even among the 60,000 Allied POWS, the Dutch and British considerably outnumbered the Australians. About twenty percent of them died, especially after the notorious 'Speedo' was implemented in April 1943.

In her Foreword to Arch and Martin Flanagan's *The Line,* yet another member of that most remarkable of families, Jo Flanagan, writes this:

> Our generation holds the job of remembering, because too many of the old diggers have gone into what Dad calls 'the shadows' and now we're the ones who cling to these stories. We hold the job because, in my father's words, those men died filthy, sick, hungry, and homesick and it would be a terrible thing if they were forgotten. We hold the job because memory is our only defence against repeating the misery of history.

I agree. The Death Railway should occupy as prominent a place within the national imaginary as Gallipoli and the WWI battlefields of the Western Front. I despair that this will ever be so, Richard Flanagan's magisterial Man Booker winning novel, *The Narrow Road to the Deep North,* notwithstanding. The children of the line grew up with an implicit recognition of each other, absorbing their generational responsibility to the memory of the past.

But I am not a nationalist. I identify only as Tasmanian, and regard the notion of the nation as fraught and dubious, susceptible to knavery and manipulation, and even as a mere constitutional figment. This is why the focus of my obsession with memory is narrower, fixing upon the 2/40th Battalion, overwhelmingly Tasmanian, sent to defend an airfield on Timor with obsolete equipment, vastly outnumbered, and with no air support. Sitting ducks. In terms of military strategy it was utter madness – almost certainly deliberately sacrificial, an operation designed to fail but, it was surely hoped, to buy a little time. In this sense it was Tasmania's WW2 equivalent of Gallipoli. In its brief operational life the 2/40th achieved an extraordinary victory, destroying an entrenched Japanese position in a bayonet charge thought by some to have been the last full-battalion bayonet charge in military history – though Peter Henning thinks this unlikely (my father's own bayonet charge, mentioned earlier, was a discrete charge within the larger charge). Arch Flanagan was not in the 2/40th, and was not captured in Timor. Tom Uren was not in the 2/40th either, but he was in Timor, with the 2/1st Heavy Battery, and his Bren carrier provided cover for the Tasmanians advancing up Oesoe Ridge. In *The Fight*, Martin Flanagan quotes Uren as saying, softly: 'The 2/40th were a wonderful battalion. A lot of them were killed but they took the ridge. I thought the whole Anzac thing was phoney bullshit up til then'.

The 2/40th 'family' has now become the sons and daughters of the returned men, the generation that now seeks to preserve the memory of those Sally Dingo calls 'magnificent ordinary men'. Sally grew up on the North-West Coast, in a town not far from my own. In *Unsung Ordinary Men: A Generation Like No Other,* she writes of the strangeness she felt growing up when she was in 'the houses of families whose fathers had not been prisoners of the Japanese. In fact, I hardly knew what to say when I was in such houses'. Quite so. I remember talking this over with her – and of her remarking how the children of returned men recognised each other in school and street. How we just knew.

But that was then and now is now. Not all 2/40th men ended up on the Death Railway after capture, but most did. In an important way, then, the Railway is part of the Tasmanian story – not exclusively, but a significant component thereof notwithstanding. And now we, the generation of memory keepers, is growing old in turn. I cannot control the island's myth-construction processes. And I fear.

*

The line from Hellfire Pass up to the national park has been reconstituted as a walking track, ending at Compressor Cutting, 2.5 hours away. To continue walking from the end of the made walking track would be a shorter tramp to Jungle Camp No. 1 than the trek down from Kinsaiyok that I had attempted. I must bear that in mind. Meanwhile, Matt and his party set out on the hike from Hellfire Pass. I have a day pack, a very light one – but the fit and powerful Mai Tai adepts won't allow me to carry it.

We pass through gorge country, and here the Railway's construction required a dangerous series of cuttings and frail, spindly bridges, six of the latter before Hintok Station was reached. Today, though, we aren't supposed to get that far. 1.5 hours of walking brings us to Hintok Road, paved, straight and somehow demeaning in its brash modernity. Here is our bus, and here we are meant to stop, for a storm has trashed the bamboo beyond the intersecting road, and a sign prohibits entry. We haven't made it to Hintok. But now cousin Matt does a strange and courageous thing – 'courageous' given that the Thai military controls this land. He asks me whether I want to go on. Of course I do. So do we all. We squeeze through the wire, pick and batter a path through the fallen bamboo, and thus we make it to Hintok, interpretive signage still weirdly in place in the wrecked jungle. And I am satisfied.

Now the bus heads for Bangkok and beyond, to the martial arts gym where big and strong Australians spar with and receive instruction from supple young Thais half their size. But that's another story.

Murphy versus Descartes – *Domum Invenio, Ergo Sum*

(Written c.2009 and published in 2016 in *Professorial Paws: Dogs in Scholars' Lives' and Work*, Ardra Cole and Sharon Sbrocchi eds, Backalong Books, Halifax NS; and 2019 in *The Sky Falls Down: An Anthology of Loss*, Terry Whitebeach and Gina Mercer eds, Ginninderra Press, Port Adelaide, SA.)

As a young Australian academic I was employed on what was then called a 'greenfields' campus: a small – intimately small – quasi-university (a 'College of Advanced Education') new-built within a grove of hoary macrocarpa on an erstwhile dairy farm outside a small rural city. I was deeply insecure. No-one in my large extended family had even attended an institution of tertiary education, let alone gone on to teach in one. Insecure, then – but outspoken, aggressive, articulate (within that context). Among my colleagues I suffered no incompetence, though I knew myself to be the most bumbling of fools, even within that assemblage of academic misfits. I was, by contrast, unfailingly considerate and patient towards those who struggled in my classes (that, at least, was my determined intent).

To this place of intellectual employ came, each day, my border collie cross, Murphy.

I would pull up in the windswept carpark, routinely note the dreary monotony of the flat, dun, cypress-dominated vista and the functionality of the new campus buildings, trudge past the crumbling sandstone base of the farm's old watertank – it must have been an extraordinary edifice in its day – and slosh through red lava-flow mud to the main building.

With Murphy at heel. At the door she would proffer her day's farewell and trot, in her beautiful prance, her white-tipped tail bannering jauntily, back to the carpark. There she reigned, queen of the campus. She was the wise and gentle spirit that constituted this unlikely place a unity. There weren't many of us, staff or students, in this raw landscape with its scarcely-hallowed halls, and Murphy knew us all. Students who had no dealings with me joyously called her name, stopped and communed with her. She was an institution, and much loved. Much more loved than prickly young me, and with a wider circle of acquaintance.

She was also illegal.

Small my campus may have been, but that was no protection against the pernickety pettiness of bureaucracy. At regular intervals a memo would do the rounds, reminding staff that they were not to bring their dogs to work. It was aimed at me — but its author, presumably not wanting to tackle me head-on, generalised and broadcast it. It didn't work — I would reply with as much pompous acerbity as I could muster, calling the memo's author a 'wee tim'rous beastie', suggesting that he should try to grow a spine and talk to me personally, and informing him that, until then, I would treat his instruction with contempt. There would be no response, the edict would be ignored as promised, and months later the entire charade would be replayed. I must have been insufferable. The wonder of it is that I have so many dear and lasting friends from that time.

*

I hold certain minority views about academic pedagogy, though they are, I am gratified to observe, now deemed much less heretical than they once were.

I have spent a long and satisfying academic career as a sort of a stateless person – 'stateless' in the sense that I call no discipline my 'home'. I was trained in political science, but only at the beginning of my career did I actually work in a department / school of political science / government. For the rest I was employed in academic enclaves that were proudly trans-disciplinary, and which suffered acute discrimination on that account. I came to believe in trans-disciplinarity – to believe, indeed, that the disciplines are useful paradigms for the organisation of knowledge only at the most basic level, beyond which they become a serious constraint upon intellectual progress. I couldn't even call myself an all-purpose social scientist or a non-specific scholar of the humanities, moving, as I did, seamlessly between the two.

And I have long contested the convention within academic publishing that forbids deployment of the perpendicular pronoun. The fiction is, the name(s) below the title notwithstanding, that the paper has somehow managed to write itself. This has always seemed to me to be utterly cowardly – to enable the author to hide from view; to eschew responsibility for his/her scholarship. It is time to put this iniquitous fiction out to pasture – as, indeed, has largely occurred now within the humanities, though it remains tenacious in the social sciences, and supremely unchallenged in the physical sciences. I have bristled over this for more than a quarter of a century, and it will be a day of joy when there is no longer a need to argue it out with journal editors.

I do, of course, know the origin of the convention that academic writing should be depersonalised. It stems from the abrupt split between subject and object that is one of the most potent legacies of the Age of Enlightenment in general, and Cartesian dualism in particular. For Descartes, the radical separation of subject and object was the principle that cleared the decks for scientific inquiry, the epistemological mode that would set humankind on a trajectory of endless, technology-fueled progress, truly rendering us 'masters and possessors of nature'. The 'subject' – he who would know (it was emphatically a 'he' in Descartes' day) – is radically separate from, emotionally remote from, and unaffected (or 'uncontaminated') by the 'object' – that concerning which knowledge is sought. It is from Descartes that we derive the fundamental principle of the scientific method – the notion of the sanitised experiment in which the scientist dispassionately 'interrogates', 'dissects' and 'reduces' the experiment's 'object'.

Well, okay. I'm neither anti-science nor in the front row of its cheerleaders. But Descartes didn't stop there. For him dualism was a universal principle, not just an epistemological device.

Not merely perceptual: a separation of observing subject from observed object. It also separated, in a fundamental way, that small component of the brain responsible for rational thought (in Descartes' understanding of human anatomy) from the rest. Humans think. In the act of thought they live. *Cogito, ergo sum* – 'I think, therefore I am' – the best known of the Cartesian aphorisms. Not, 'I cry, therefore I am'. Not 'I run, therefore I am'. I think. If I do not think, I do not exist. Literally. Only the thinking brain is truly alive, truly immortal. The rest of the human body is mere machine, functioning in accordance with certain God-derived mechanical principles.

And then there are the animals. Which don't think. Only humans think, and, thus, only humans have souls, these being synonymous. Animals have no share in immortality; no soul. They are *entirely* machine, acting, Descartes tells us in Part 5 of the *Discourse on Method*, 'according to the arrangement of their organs, just as we see how a clock, composed merely of springs and wheels, can reckon the hours'. And they do not feel pain. As I have written elsewhere (of the Cartesian paradigm): 'as only the soul, the living part of existence, can experience pain – mere machines cannot do that – it follows that animals can feel no pain'. But how can that be? Animals seem to emit the sounds we associate with experiencing pain. Ah, no. Such apparent expressions of pain (again borrowing from myself) actually 'have the status of the discordant noises that emanate from any faulty or damaged machine'.

My dogs – not just Murphy: also Dougal, my shrewd and loving little canine fluffy slipper; my second border collie cross, timid, bewildered Duffy; gentle, curly-haired Bill; and feisty, grey Flossie – prised me loose from this way of thinking. Descartes should have had a dog – as a companion, not an experimental 'object'. He would have come to understand that in dogs exist the same variation in intelligence and personality, and ingenuity in communication and problem-solving, as are to be found in humans. To observe the complexity of a dog's cognition as it manifests in subtleties of behaviour and mood is to render ludicrous the notion that here is a mere machine, functioning according to strict mechanical principles.

Descartes' own lame explanation for demonstrations of intelligence in animals was that these are matched, in the same animal, by demonstrations of stupidity; and that, besides, only humans possess the gift of speech. Let's take this matter of 'shows of intelligence'. I'd already long since lost truck with this argument when I read, not many years ago, Mary Midgley's marvellous book, *Beast and Man* (written in 1979, though I read it in Routledge's 1995 revised edition). Midgley exposes the partiality of Descartes' 'standard' of intelligence'. 'People', she writes:

> are also capable of acting both intelligently and stupidly, and relatively stupid conduct by a fairly intelligent being on an off-day is not in the least like the 'stupidity' of a machine. A car cannot even try to find its way home; a clock will not make even a bad shot at identifying danger. Stupid solutions [at least] show a consciousness of the problem.

Brilliant. Wish I'd written that. In knowing that is has to get home, and in recognising danger, a dog will show an intelligence that clearly cannot be equated with the 'intelligence' of a machine. It may, like a human, make the wrong decision in response to the problem, but in identifying the problem an intelligence is deployed that is closer to that of a human than it is to that of a machine. As for the criterion of language, this, too, is easily dispensed with, and Midgley does just that, pointing out that science itself has now shown that 'language, or the power to speak it, is actually not the unsplittable, single, unmistakable thing people had supposed'.

I could never have identified the problem with the Cartesian distinction as forensically as Midgley has. But just now my two current dogs, Flossie and boisterous, mischievous Ollie, have scampered, nimble-footed, along the very edge of the sea-cliff just down from the shanty in which I am writing. I hold my breath. One false step and that's it for them. But there isn't a false step, of course, just as there never was for their predecessors. Few humans could do this, though. Why do we valorise complexity of speech and thought instead of this ability? Aren't we being just a tad self-serving? The cheetah can run faster than any living creature. Why does this not entitle the cheetah to claim the species championship of the world? Isn't it just a little disingenuous to fasten upon the one activity in which humans seem so plainly superior to all other species and claim this as *the* criterion upon which claims to superiority objectively lodge?

So it was that I left the Cartesian paradigm behind and went in search of more grounded theories of knowledge, of explanations for emotional and bodily intelligence, of systems of ethics based within notions of a democracy of species and the primacy of ecological relationships. Phenomenology rather than positivism. The indeterminacy and flux of the new physics rather than the rigid certainties of mechanistic, old-paradigm science. The subject as research informant – subject and object in dynamic interplay – rather than emotionally remote, 'uncontaminated' investigation. Story and description in synergy with, rather than precluded by, analysis. At the heart of these choices – big important choices – lies the quiet wisdom of Murphy the border collie, and Dougal the bichon-westy, and their deep, complex companionship. I loved them then and I love them still, and they will walk beside me now as I take my beachcomber's constitutional around Killora Bay.

*

All this is knowledge registered and absorbed within my brain – even the understanding that the entire body and all the senses contribute to knowing was a cerebral understanding. But I also became aware of sub-rational modes of knowing through interaction with my dogs. Much of this occurs sub-linguistically – it is the sort of communication that takes place when a dog locks eyes with you, holds your gaze and concentrates meaning into that gaze. It is a mode of communication that, at best, proceeds by suggestion and hint, persistently reminding you how deep the gulf that separates the species, how emphatic the deficit in cross-species understanding. It is, nevertheless, my window – my misted-over window – into the essence of animal being.

But dog-human communication is not entirely sub-linguistical. There is compelling evidence that the dog, the first species to be domesticated, developed its barking range to communicate with us, and that we developed a commensurate vocal range to make our needs known to them. This included the precise communication needed for herding, for without the dog we would have remained hunter-gatherers. It may not be going too far to observe that the development of the symbiotic relationship between humans and dogs was a necessary prerequisite to civilisation itself, and that, as a consequence, dogs and humans are uniquely attuned to each other, their understanding of each other superior, probably, than that between humans and chimpanzees, our closest genetic relatives.

Do I talk to my dogs, then? Absolutely – and they talk to me. It is a primal communication, sometimes fraught, the capacity for misunderstanding ever-present, especially when vocal communication is mixed with that more ineffable communication that transpires through the silent locking of eyes. There are those who are critical of dogs – even antagonistic towards them – because the dog is seen to be incompatible with the principle of, and the presence of, the wild. The late Australian philosopher,

Val Plumwood, took this view. And it is undeniably true that to be in the bush with a dog is to greatly reduce one's chances of significant encounters with wild creatures. But, as briefly thrilling as such encounters can be, their 'significance' is mostly tenuous – it is the thrill of the voyeur, and not to be compared with the deep, electric, uncertain window into animal being that I take from canine communication. 'With friends like this who needs enemies? Bah, humbug', writes David Quammen in his mean-spirited essay, 'The Descent of the Dog'. Quammen may be the most perceptive of men on most of the topics on which he chooses to write, but on matters canine he simply doesn't get it.

*

Occasionally I'd forget Murphy. As one forgets one's shadow. I'd drive across town to play sport, say, and I'd let her out of the car to nose about and explore the ground. Then I'd get back in the car and drive home. An hour or so later Murphy would turn up, having successfully negotiated her way across and past busy freeways and dog-catchers. Domum invenio, ergo sum - *I can find my way home, therefore I am.*

Once, when she was very old – she lived to almost 20 – it took her a day to get home, and she was spent. I was thoroughly irresponsible. I did not do well at her death either, nor at that of loyal, quizzical Dougal. I know they'd forgive me, but that's no comfort, and I live with the guilt of having been found wanting in their hour of need, after all they'd selflessly given me. The last and hardest wisdom gifted me by my soft-eyed companions is this: how easy it is, in the juggle of life's pulls and its pushes, to act with an innocent shoddiness towards others. Murphy, Dougal, Duffy and those who now run in their stead taught me the complexity of relational ethics, and the struggle to do right by others that is the measure of an honourable life.

Painting the Shape of the Wind - Pattern and Chaos in the Island Art of Sue Lovegrove.

(This is a shortened version of an essay originally published in *Artlink*, 32[1], 2012.)

If you head for Pelverata on one of those great old roads, winding and unsealed, that still abound off Tassie's beaten track, if you travel this road away from the lush river flats of the Huon River and into the western foothills of the Snug Tiers, you will come to an unpainted house of simple design, steeply gabled. It sits in paddocks backed by dry sclerophyll forest with *E. ovata* dominant, rich habitat for eastern barred bandicoots, Tasmanian native hens, eastern quolls and *healthy* Tasmanian devils, as well as the obligatory abundance of wallabies and brushies. Here, on 20 acres of 'horrible clay', Sue Lovegrove lives and works. Her house, indeed, is a large, expansive studio.

Sue roamed the continent before washing out in these Tasmanian hills, since when she has become an island painter. I do not mean Tasmania – I mean smaller, outrigger islands where the wind weaves pattern and chaos – simultaneously – from light, water, reed and dune grass. Sue was an Antarctic Arts Fellow, and she stopped over at Macquarie Island. She was an artist-in-residence on cliff-walled Maatsuyker Island off Tasmania's wild south coast. She has taken her easel to Egg Island, an elongated, species-rich riverine island in the Huon River. And as I write, she is planning and packing for Tasman Island, also sheer-walled, but standing beneath the commanding presence of Cape Pillar and the highest sea-cliffs – they do say – in the Southern Hemisphere. Sue Lovegrove has been here three times as a WildCare weeder, but this trip is 'all art'. Not that she failed to put her earlier visits to good creative purpose. At the time of writing her latest exhibition, *Glimpse*, is hanging in Gallerysmith in North Melbourne. This is the latest instalment in *The Shape of the Wind* series, and it explores, she tells me, 'the patterning and rhythms of the island through the complex linear structure of the island's grasses'.

An interest in white, the default colour of space, took Lovegrove to Antarctica, and it is a thread that remains within the weave of her work. White became its base colour, though you need to look deep within some of the paintings to realise this. White *is* the wind. It is there, in semi-transparent layers that let the image through, even in the later grass-dense paintings. Light and air and expansiveness predominate. Even as the gaze upon light and cloud came to be populated by cross-cut intersections of grass, the one echoed the other. The lines are to do with how you feel the air – how grass might brush across your face.

On Macquarie Island Sue encountered herbfields and meadows of grass – but no trees. It was as if the bones of the living island had been bared to the scrutiny of space. On elemental Maatsuyker Island, where she lived 'a monastic life', the artist 'talked to the island as if it was a living thing'. She moved from what she calls 'cloudwork' to painting 'the belly of the island – the dark damp vegetation'. It was, she says, a process of 'leaving ice behind and finding grass', a process that seems to have begun with her encounter with those intricate and infinitely complex microworlds of the Macquarie Island herbfields and grasslands. Now she travels 'looking at the grass. Some people look at the view – I look down to where the lichens are, and the little creatures that no-one sees.' In these microworlds, worlds entire unto themselves, worlds of endless, distilled complexity, the shape of the wind finds delineation, its white dance taking on tints of delicate, mute colour, a play of warm and cool so subtle that you don't realise what you are seeing. And as it is, so she paints.

For this transition the artist sought a visual language of grass, one that can convey dimensions deep beyond surfaces – abstraction, but not so abstract that the subject becomes a purely cerebral event.

There is tension, too, between the white depth of space and the detailing line – also white – that the grass supplies. She wants the eye to flicker from surface to inner deep to surface to inner deep. On first encountering Sue Lovegrove's work my eye tended to stop at the flat of the surface, seeing each canvas as alike to a photographic close-up. I soon came to realise the inadequacy of this, but it is true that the opacity of white makes it difficult to use, and it is a challenge to achieve a sense of depth. She shows me the painting she deems her best – *The Shape of the Wind No. 495* – and I see, or rather half see, the dynamism she achieves through the weave of lines and the hint of pattern within the apparently random that lies at the heart of things – what the physicist, David Bohm, called 'implicate order'. It is an aesthetics of the glimpse – of things not gazed at, but held at the edge of perception, half seen, half intuited, but palpably there.

Sue Lovegrove seeks to convey the emergence of implicate pattern within the chaotic complexity of the life of her wind-shaped, unpeopled islands. She has devised a way of working to fit her intent. She paints on the floor of her home/studio, completely immersed, working the painting up in tiny, soft lines of gouache, using an extremely small brush. She strokes the canvas into life, the end product taking its rhythm from the rhythms of the process. If it's not to her liking, 'I take it down the paddock and hose it down with rain water. It doesn't all come off, it leaves a ghost. Lines sit over it. And the canvas itself acquires a story.' The painting slowly emerges, and within the painting a pattern, ephemeral, glimpsed at the edge of the eye, also emerges, lurking within the chaotic complexity of crosscutting lines. It is a tension in the scheme of things – a tension between the pattern of self-organising systems that constitute living organisms and entire ecosystems, and the disorder, the pizzazz, in the chaos of its endlessly varying morphologies. Just now Lovegrove seeks to paint these tensions within the complexity of Tasman Island's wind-moulded grasslands. You take the landscape inside yourself, she says, 'feel its pattern inside your body' – and thus you learn to paint the shape of the wind.

'The Pulp' – Reflections on an Island Dreaming

(First published as 'Tassie Is Far from Run-of-the-Mill', a 'Saturday Soapbox' article in *The Mercury*, 25 August 2012. *Last Days of the Mill*, published by Forty South Publishing, was shortlisted for the 2013 Tasmanian Book Prize, and won the People's Choice Award.)

In 2012 I teamed up with visual artist, Tony Thorne, to write a book about the 2010 closure of the Burnie pulp mill – 'The Pulp'.

Tony, an animator of global prominence (his credits include the Harry Potter and Happy Feet movies) is a Burnie boy, now quietly domiciled in Hobart. He went onto the mill floor on The Pulp's very last day of operation to visually record that momentous event. And I arrived in Burnie shortly afterwards with my trusty digital recorder, all set to gather stories and opinions about a town faced with the task of re-inventing itself. Prominent among my interviewees was a cohort of workers from the mill floor. Tony and I pooled our labours and *Last Days of the Mill* was subsequently born.

Why did we do it? A legitimate question. Why did its launch in Hobart – a long way from Burnie – fill a bookshop to the gun'ls?

For this reason. The closure of the Burnie mill was not simply the demise of yet another Tasmanian enterprise left behind by technological change and the capricious flows of global capital. This was an event that powerfully symbolises Tasmania's shift from an obsolete political economy to something distinctively new, the contours of which are still not firmly established.

The great Tasmanian dreaming, tracing back to the first decades of the twentieth century, was one in which the island at the end of the earth would become a throbbing, roaring engine of heavy industry, an island of clamour and smokestacks, the Ruhr Valley of the southern seas, all made possible through the medium of endless, cheap hydro power. It was a heroic aspiration, eventually realised only in part, and best viewed in the context of its tangible emblems – the mines of the West Coast, the smelters on the Tamar, the textile mills in Launceston, the zinc works on the Derwent, and two pulp mills, one at either end of the island. Among these, the promise and ultimate shortcomings of the great dreaming were most potently embodied in the pulp mill at Burnie, and nothing is more dramatically symbolic of the rift between Tasmania's old industrial economy and the island's emergence into a post-industrial world than the closing of 'The Pulp'.

Our heroic industrial dreaming was socially inclusive and politically bipartisan, an article of faith so apparently self-evident and so universally shared that it floated below scrutiny and dispute.

In keeping with the social inclusivity of the vision, APPM Burnie was socially responsible. It carried a workforce far larger than its own economic interests would have dictated, and it provided its employees with an extraordinarily generous range of sporting, health, housing and welfare services and facilities.

As the western world turned away from compassion in the bleak 80s, embracing instead an arid economic rationalism, so too did the pulp mill, now under the rationalist management of North Broken Hill. A gulf opened between management and workforce and mistrust flourished, culminating in the bitter, nationally important industrial dispute of 1992. From there it was all downhill. Again under new management, the mill rapidly downsized, and so did the town, shedding a fifth of its population in the 1990s. We were slow to appreciate it, but this, too, was a development in lockstep with trends throughout the western world.

Burnie is now constructing new meanings for itself and discovering civic capacities that had long remained dormant while the benevolent largesse of the company prevailed. There are many in Burnie who see only disaster in the closing of the mill, the displaced mill workers themselves prominently among them. There are others who see the closure of the mill as liberatory, an unlocking of the town's slumbering potential. In this, Burnie symbolises the island. The old dreaming has run its course, and an uncertain future beckons. The coming of the Greens emblemises this change, but it is a change that would have happened had the Greens never existed, because Tasmania's changing political economy merely holds a mirror to economic tides that are sweeping the western world.

The new economy will be more mindful of environmental values, and for that we can be grateful. But there will be losers, people whose skills and values were honed within the economy that is passing, and who lack the resilience to make the necessary transition. They deserve acknowledgement. The mill floor of The Pulp had a rich and unique culture, with work practices specific to the mill. It generated an endless trove of story. It even generated linguistic idiosyncracies specific to that one workplace.

Tony and I determined that these working lives should not be allowed to vanish into the recesses of aging memories, thence into oblivion. The workers of the Burnie pulp mill lived at the heart of the dreaming that went unchallenged in the island for very many decades. Their stories, their unique way of being Tasmanian, needed, we thought, to be honoured. That is what we set out to do.

To Tilt at Windmills, and so Change the World

(First published as a catalogue essay for the exhibition, *Giving Voice: The Art of Dissent*, curated by Yvonne Rees-Pagh for the Salamanca Arts Centre, Hobart, August-September 2014.)

People have died, nobly and bravely, to achieve democracy. They have died all over the world and over many centuries. In the affluent west, the twentieth century was smugly trumpeted as the 'democratic century', and a democratic trajectory within the grand tides of human affairs was assumed to be the essential vector of history.

But it is clear that no such vector exists, and we are in the process of a monumental betrayal. We are betraying those who fought and died to achieve democracy. Democracy – that state of public affairs in which all people have meaningful access and input to the making of those decisions to which they are thereafter subject – is fleeing from us; seeping through the cracks of our collective existence. We are both architects of and careless witnesses to this tragedy.

In part democracy is slipping from us because political power is ungraspable. People seek election to parliament in the belief that they can then make a difference. In a small way, they can. But I have worked for politicians, and I know that in their more reflective moments they puzzle over their own apparent powerlessness. Even the President of the United States, who I once thought the most powerful person in the world, I now deem to be the front man (always, to date, a man) for an amorphous committee of power, his hands in large part tied by the cumbersome inertia of the subterranean workings of that inchoate web. Power is everywhere, and it is nowhere. This being so, it is unmonitorable. And those who really do cling to an aspect of it are able to rort and gouge within the confines of that small market they have cornered, below the blunted public gaze, and invisibly subversive of the democratic realm.

And, too, democracy emerged as a form of government suitable for a simpler time. It was appropriate to a certain level of technological development, back when we could realistically expect to grasp the ins-and-outs of any political issue and understand the consequences attaching to each option. We have left those times behind. In large part our lives are technologically moulded. The determinations of most profound significance in shaping the conditions within which we live are decisions for investment in the development and implementation of new technologies. Except occasionally, when clear ethical or religious principles are thought to be at stake (such as stem-cell research) these decisions are not subject to democratic scrutiny or deliberation; they are not determined within public forums. The first we know of them is when they lob into our lives. Of course, *all* these developments have ethical consequences – and much else besides. Choices to develop or not develop new technologies, though, require a technical sophistication that is beyond most citizens, and beyond most politicians. Here is another reason why political power slides away from democratic oversight – its technical complexity makes it democratically unmanageable; unassessable, and, ultimately, invisible. And in the absence of a democratic brake we are driven along by a technological determinism. The logic of technological 'drive' is that what can be done will be done.

A third factor in the white-anting of democracy is the political intelligensia's love affair with economic liberalism (paradoxically labelled 'conservatism' in the strange terms of American politic-speak). Economic and political liberalisms were allies in the struggle to free humans from the traditional shackles of aristocratic and ecclesiastical oligarchy in the eighteenth and nineteenth centuries, but we have since seen economic liberalism turn against democracy; to anoint the imperious god of the market at the expense of democratic institutions. The implications of this are not well understood, so I'll spell them out. To hand political decision-making to the market is to turn thinking, reflective, self-actualising citizens into mindless zombies reacting reflexively (not reflectively) to market signals. Though its zealots will tell you otherwise, the market is profoundly undemocratic, because people do not have equal access to the market and its determinations. Those with buying power – the affluent – have many, many more 'votes' in the market than those without, and corporate institutions have the most market votes of all. To those who have, the market endlessly gives more. It is undemocratic, then, and in its reduction of the self-actualising citizen to the mindlessly Pavlovian consumer its tendency is totalitarian, and there's a contradiction for you – the morphing, in the times in which we live, of the liberal tradition into a form of totalitarianism!

There are other pathologies. One is the essentially Stalinist nature of the political party as a very institution, demanding, as it does, an uncritical group-think on the part of its faithful. Another is the treason of the fourth estate – the mass media – no longer fear-nought and neutral in its commitment to truth and to the exposure of wrongs, but increasingly the mouthpiece of the rich and powerful whose advertising dollars pay their dividends and their salaries. At its worst you get that debasement of once lofty principles that renders News Limited's Australian flagship, *The Australian*, a craven propaganda sheet for the Liberal Party. Yet another pathology of democracy is the systemic corruption of those who attain a small corner of power. As Lord Acton – a Conservative! – observed, power does indeed corrupt, and absolute power corrupts absolutely. Or it may be that, having obtained office, what is discovered is the earlier-noted disconnect between the trappings of power and the illusion of power. You have been elected – and still you remain powerless when it comes to resolving seemingly intractable problems. Perhaps this explains why those elected turn instead to substitute activities. To systematically trashing the natural world. To obscene self-enrichment. To appalling acts of state-sponsored terrorism. To wage war against one's own people while brazenly claiming a democratic mandate.

What is to be done? Those who fought and died to end tyranny; to install in its place a mode of making public decisions called 'democracy' – what do we owe those people? Is 'democracy' destined to ever remain a fraudulent but potent concept trotted out to legitimise authority in the real world, but really an unattainable ideal?

We need answers to these questions and I don't have them. No single person does, because the virtue of democracy lodges in its vision of open-access, collective synergies from which legitimate decisions emerge. I don't have answers, but I know that disengagement is not an option. Mindless consumerism is not an option. Citizenship must be re-invented, and asserted. In particular we must find a way to bring technological 'drive' under democratic control – to make determinations of technological investment subject to public process. And we must not forget that great aphorism: 'All that is necessary for the triumph of evil is that good men [and women] do nothing'. Do you know who said that? Who the fire-breathing lefty was who coined those words? Well that great flash of political wisdom comes down to us from Edmund Burke, another Conservative. The struggle for a reinvented, robust and viable democratic realm should be non-partisan.

These observations lead to an incontrovertible observation. The future of democratic institutions lies outside the system and in the realm of activism. The negative feedback supplied by outside-the-system activism is democracy's most vital component. This is something Tasmania's Liberal Government should take sharp notice of as it prepares legislation to divest itself of the inconvenience of activism's negative feedback! Reform needs to take us in the opposite direction – but those within the corrupted institutions and processes of the formal system have too much to lose to do that. They will continue to try to tell us that democracy is hale as long we vote for Tweedledum or Tweedledee at an election every few years, after which we can forget about citizenship until the next inconvenient democracy-for-a-day event rolls around.

No, democracy will be refashioned from within the realms of dissent, if it is to be rescued at all.

This does not come easily, and many doomed tilts at windmills will be required along the way. It may be that a contemplated act has no prospect of achieving a successful outcome. But if it is the *right* thing to do, it should be done – and who is to say that it will not have a ramifying impact.

Art in the Forgotten Corners – The Photojournalism of Matthew Newton

(Originally the text of a talk at the opening of Matthew Newton's exhibition, *Another Country*, Artspace, April 2014. A revised version was subsequently published on *TasmanianTimes.com*)

I'm the best person to open this exhibition. Because among my lesser-known art credits is this: I have spent many hours, in many strange places, serving an apprenticeship as a photographer's go-fetch; a photographer's dogsbody. And this apprenticeship was served in the demanding employ of none other than this man – Matt Newton. Or 'Matthew' Newton as he prefers to call himself professionally – for mysterious reasons best known to the man himself.

I'm reminded of a day on the Huon River. Matt's taking photos: portrait shots of, I think, the Huon Environment Centre's Jenny Webber. And Muggins here is his lighting gopher. So we're there on the banks of the river, and I'm holding the light-pole, and I look down and the river's right there – and it's black and sinister, it's racing along, and it's bottomless. And Newty says, 'Hazy, just take a step back'. And I say what's bleeding obvious: 'mate, if I go back a step, the last you'll see of me is my hat racing off to Huonville'. To which Newty ripostes: 'it's times like this, mate, when you find out who's really prepared to go the extra yard for their art'.

Well I thought, yes, that's all very well, but it's not actually my art for which I'm being asked to make the ultimate sacrifice. I suck it down, though. Scowl. Put on my disgusted face. And Newty gives in – though for the rest of the day the vindictive bastard continues, at every available opportunity, to have me standing up to my hocks in freezing mountain water.

But – back to the point of this story. That stuff about taking one for your *art*.

Now, Newts is a photojournalist – the finest exponent of his craft in Tasmania and close to being the finest in the country. A few years back his photo essay on the forest blockades in the Weld and the Florentine went within an ace of landing him the Walkley. This very year he was shortlisted for the National Portrait Prize. Within his genre, the man is a heavy hitter.

Righto. So here we are in *Arts* Tasmania's fine shopfront gallery, *Art*space. But is what Newty does really *art*? Can you be a photojournalist *and* an artist?

The first thing you should know is that we are not supposed to use the word 'photojournalist' these days. 'Documentary photographer' is now the preferred term, and the reason for this is that the latter is thought somehow to elide the difference between art and mere recordage – though for the life of me I can't see how it does that. Whatever you call it, it seems to me that the tradition in which Newty sits is one in which an image-maker 'strives' – these are not my words – 'strives to be an objective recorder of real events, and thus, they don't meddle with their pictures'. In her classic work on photography's standing as art, *On Photography,* Susan Sontag famously made the case that the superiority of photography as a visual medium lodges within its intrinsic truthfulness. 'The camera doesn't lie', we always used to say.

We now know that that's crap. With the coming of digital technologies the manipulative capacity of the photographic image has expanded exponentially. So, insofar as documentary photography is 'concerned with the truth of the image as an objective marker of the moment' – again, not my words – it seeks to remain true to an older, simpler, one might even say 'old-fashioned' idea of photography. One in which there would not seem to be much scope for the creative expressiveness that marks artistic endeavour.

And it is in *this* tradition that Matt Newton works. We could justifiably conclude, then, that this man might be a craftsman, but, as a mere recorder, a mere documenter, he is not an artist – and Arts Tasmania's gallery space should never have been given over to him.

Well – we would, of course, be wrong if we thought that.

I want to bring two ideas together. The first is that this sort of photography is inherently *engaged*, inherently *political*. It confronts – and it just *does* this; this function is built into the very essence of the enterprise. And the second is that it has the ability both to be precise – its recording function – *and to contain an echo of something larger*. And it is in this latter capacity that it crosses into the realm of art. In my view Sontag's observation remains relevant – when the camera's lens probes beneath the prosaic surface of things, it can, if it is in the hands of an adept, a *visionary,* penetrate to truths and essences that can only be touched by the non-rational, ineffable processes of art. Art and radical change agendas in the real world thereby come potently together. When its potential is realised, the camera takes us to the *un*-posed, the *un*-framed, the *un*-rehearsed – down there, *in* there, where shining nuggets of truth and beauty elusively lodge.

And this is what Matt Newton does. He observes, he looks deeply inward, and he finds the diamantine purity in the soul of a person, a place, or a fraught, anguished event.

He does that here, in these images. He takes us – he tells us so himself – into 'another country', the island's forgotten corners, with their forgotten people. He looks beyond the cute and beautiful flash on the surface of things. And there, behind the faux tourist prettiness, he finds a deeper, more tenacious beauty. I've been in the bush with Newty. I've been down the Franklin with him. And I know that his senses are tuned to beauty. The deeper truths to which Matt Newton's documentary *art* penetrates can be grim. They can be tough – and they can still be beautiful. They capture the unbearable, ennobling beauty that alleviates even the most dour contest for existence.

These images take us out of Hobart into the island's distinctive and forgotten corners – forgotten, that is, by we who live in Hobart. We encounter the dignity of *Moonbird Boy*; the knockabout comfort of high country shacks under winter snow; the appalling sadness of a net-caught, callously disposed of, baby dolphin; the sudden emergent shock of a devil on King's Run (that was another of my photographer's dogsbody excursions); we see the uncomfortable beauty of a storm raging in on the Roaring Forties to pummel Trial Harbour; the quiet endurance of the Zeehan 'Peace Horse'; the spectacular rust colours of the Iron Blow, in startling juxtaposition with prosaic country dwellings; deer antlers incongruously – or *is* it incongruously? – contrasting with the red cross of mercy. A man of vision and deft technique is at work here in the island's quiet corners. A man who searches for the elusive essence of the very island. The man treats his volunteer labour like shit, but put a camera in his hand and he's a genius.

The Breath of Vast Time

(First published on-line in *Cordite*, 44 [*Gondwanaland* issue]. The poetry excerpts come from the following sources, in the order in which they appear in the essay: 'In Memory of William Paterson...', *Silently On The Tide*; 'Lost in Rainforest, King William Range', *The View from the Non-Members' Bar*; 'On the Gordon River Cruise: Notes for a Poem', *Silently On The Tide*; 'Lost in Rainforest, King William Range', *The View from the Non-Members' Bar*; 'Old Man's Beard', *Island*.)

'May the future make shift for itself.
I would know how it was before...'

I sit in Kevin Kiernan's garden on the middle slopes of The Mountain. In the 1970s a young Kevin Kiernan was prominent in the unsuccessful struggle to save Lake Pedder from inundation within a back-up storage reservoir, a struggle that stands within Australian history as the first battle for wilderness preservation of national eminence. Kiernan's essay from those days, 'I Saw My Temple Ransacked', remains a classic of engaged nature writing. I am here to interview him about environmental activism.

Around me are many plants that are familiar to me, the trees of the Gondwana forests. Except that they are not *entirely* familiar, because these trees are from South America, cousin species to those of our own rainforests, but so similar that the differences defy recognition unless you know what to look for. In my own place-specific engagement with Gondwana I find it easy to overlook the vast planetary ambit of the super-continent's legacy. Kevin's garden wakens me to it. I am reminded, too, of the Wollemi Pine, only 'discovered' in 1994, and in a secluded Blue Mountains ravine a little over 150 kms from Sydney its very self. This may have been the great Australian botanical discovery of the departed century. And it is a Gondwana plant – a member of the Araucarian conifer family, one deemed by some to be an evolutionary dead-end. And known to my island only from the pollen record. I must lift my eyes beyond the island's shore, for there's still a lot of Gondwana out there.

The past has always held more fascination for me than the future. The future reeks with dire portent. The past, at least, is inscribed with our evolutionary success, we who are *specifically* still here, we swimmers, fliers, crawlers, wrigglers, striders, lopers and scurriers whose genotypes and phenotypes have survived both the perils of global catastrophe and the quiet, insidious competition for those niches within which life takes hold. We have endured. The future can only be guessed at, and it must be a wild and despairing guess at that. What has already occurred, though, lies prone behind us, its record tricked out in an inchoate mix of the clear, the artlessly obscure and the deliberately obfuscated, endless puzzles to fascinate a curious mind.

I have gone too far. Who could not find the unpredictable mystery of the future as fascinating as the riddle-me incomprehensibility of the past? So I'll recast my position thus: the seamless transition of past into future is the most pressing responsibility of the body politic. This sacred trust, in short, is to carry forward the vast biological and cultural treasurehouse bequeathed by the past to the future; to chaperone history's legacy; to safeguard the passage of time; and to lodge this within the future, accessible in palimpsest, so we may know who we are, from where we have come, and, reflexively, how this shapes our new world. Anything other is a descent into the madness of an existence without identity, without agency, without context, without reference points around which to structure collective life and individual being.

This is not a plea for an end to history and change – a plea to preserve, mindlessly, the bads of the past along with its goods. Change is a simple fact. The techtonic plates will shift. Volcanic stacks will lift their lids. Continents sink, rise. Cities fall to ruin. We will deem it just that slavery ends, that women vote, that wars cease, that the young be protected from violence and predation, that same-sex couples may marry, that arid market abstractions not take precedence over the real lives of real entities, that animals be accorded ethical standing. But to have a point of moral vantage that even makes possible such determinations we need the inheritance of the past.

How far past is the past? Listen. Turn your cheek to the wind blowing from the desert, or from the seas that roll over two-thirds of the planet to wash against my island's western shores. On your cheek is the breath of vast time. The green decay of vanished forests. The foetid breath of terrible, dead lizards. Does this wind come to you out of Pangaea? That might be too big an ask. Perhaps it is even so with the great supercontinent, Gondwana, when all the lands of today's Southern Hemisphere were one, along with the Indian subcontinent and Arabian Peninsula. But the early Jurassic saw the supercontinent begin its groaning schism and East Gondwana inched away from Africa. The breath on my cheek speaks of those times.

> The forest is the sum of history:
> at the eye's edge I almost see
> looming reptiles, terrible and stark.

There is much more to Gondwana's legacy than the rainforests. But rainforest covered most of the supercontinent, and this is a legacy that endures in Australia's cool temperate forests. How should we come to these forests? On an Australian Government website I may read of ancient ferns and conifers, and 'a concentration of primitive plant families' that link directly to the evolution of flowering plants 100 million years ago. I may read that 'few places on earth contain so many plants and animals which remain relatively unchanged from their ancestors in the fossil records', and that the relic Gondwana forests are 'the most ancient type of vegetation in Australia'. That's a good start. That establishes the forests as dramatic, unique, a-fizz with portent. It leads to the illuminations of science – and I love reading the science of the forests. It may also lead to poetry.

On my island the breath of vast time blows clear, strong and charged. There is nothing fey or mystical in that observation – I write, rather, of a palpable presence; a physical fact. Gondwana concentrates here. The island is its enduring soul. Look at a map of rainforest distribution and this sense eludes – Gondwana seems a small factor on paper, strip-clinging to watercourses in Tasmania's steep, unpeopled places. Tread the ground, though, and you know you tread Gondawana. Even here, within the weak sun on my suburban deck, a pencil pine shares my space. And a strawberry pine. And a Huon pine.

The Huon pine, *Lagarostrobos franklinii,* is one of two species that, for me, emblemise Gondwana. A Tasmanian endemic, its range is confined to lakeshores and riverbanks in the wild, wet south and west. Thus it is that the vast sprawl of a super-continent distils to a precise geography. Individual Huon pines can live for 3,000 years, bested only by the bristlecone of North America. Pollen records place it on the planet 135 million years ago. It is hardcore Gondwana. At a semi-secret location near Mt. Read is a stand of genetically identical male trees with a 10,000 year old basal root stock. The tree's presence within the river systems that flow into Macquarie Harbour and Port Davey has given us stories – glorious, awful, gothically thrilling – of Sarah Island, derring-do, cannibalism, piracy. Within its resinous sap is an extraordinary oil that renders the tree almost impervious to rot, even after hundreds of years of submersion in mud. It may be the best boat building material on the planet. It buffs to a beautiful sun-capturing nutty yellow, and its scent is of the arbour of the gods. Conventionally it is said to be slow to grow, but here on my deck it springs for the sky. I once thought it unpleasing to the eye. I know better now. It sings of life's exuberance, its haphazard panache. How can such an entity not compel poetry?

> Huon pine: all scrag
> fingers from a strangler dream,
> and a heart of gold.

My other iconic rainforest species is *Nothofagus cuninghamii*, locally known as the myrtle beech, in this case a species with a range extending into Victoria. A near cousin, *Nothofagus gunnii*, restricted to the high country in the island's centre and west, has the distinction of being Tasmania's only deciduous native. Over 30 near relatives within the *Nothofagus* genus exist elsewhere in Australia, New Guinea, New Caledonia, New Zealand and South America, and even the oak and beech trees of the Northern Hemisphere are 'family'. Huon pine stands apart and unique, and is iconic to my mind on that account. The myrtle beech is iconic for the opposite reason – it is the dominant species of the Tasmanian rainforest, and if the Gondwana forests lodge within the island's soul, this is to say that in large part it is the myrtle beech that sits within the inner chamber of the island's beating heart. And it is beautiful. The foliage is small, heart-shaped, sculpted, and a deep, generous green. Excepting the new growth, which is of a burnished copper shading to red. I know of nothing like it. I have seen the autumn turning of the woods of maritime Canada. That is as glorious as it gets. For the leaf of the myrtle beech, though, another aesthetic category requires articulation. I cannot do it. Though it has drawn poetry forth in other ways:

> The gloom wraps around, patterned in
> tiny flecks of rain: time, formless,
> seeps, slides through a mess
> of lichen.

Myrtles choke in a shroud
of gnarled green parasite:
cancered logs grue and twist, aloud
with cavewet anti-light.

To find poetry in the leaf of the myrtle beech requires close engagement. And this is so, I think, of the Gondwana forests generally. The myrtle and the Huon pine might iconise the Gondwana treescape, but it is the intricate, endlessly complex microworlds within the forest that most potently enchant. I became electrically aware of this on a trip down the Franklin. As the voyage progressed I became fixated on the tiny worlds of the river bank, the never-replicated assemblages of worts, lichens, mosses, fungi, tiny flowers and herbs. It is sometimes observed that the rainforest is species-poor, and it is certainly the case that other island ecosystems harbour a greater diversity of animal life. The Gondwana forests are not, after all, Aboriginal scapes; not the product of firestick farming. Their *boundaries* may be – because the game-rich ecosystems favoured by Aboriginal peoples, open forests and grasslands, were maintained by keeping the expansionary aspirations of the Gondwana forests in check. It is even true that there is a greater floristic diversity in some other ecosystems (we might instance coastal woodlands, or low altitude wetlands). But down at the scale of the small and the infinitely intricate the proposition that the rainforests are species-poor is just not tenable. Down here with the mosses and the herbs is a window into alchemistical possibility. I come back continually to 'enchantment', because this is the word that fits. This is why I can never forgive the brutal assault upon the very soul of the island that clearfelling the Gondwana forests represents. Trees we can grow again. It is the careless disregard for the biological genius invested in the creation of those complex, irreproducible micro-worlds that I cannot forgive.

> Lichen is the forest's ancient enlightenment,
>   and the planet's —
>   and it reaches through the very fields of space
>   to infuse the cosmic winds,
> a swirl of principle
> to spark a universe.

When it comes to siting Gondwana within space I may need to lift my game — but not when it comes to that other perceptual axis, the temporal one. From the start I have known that it is that breath of vast time that has been the vector taking me from contemplation of the Gondwana forests into poetry. I love the woodlands, and I love contemplating the haunting melancholy that must have characterised the casuarina-dominated scapes after the continent dried and before the march of those brash, upstart eucalypts. But the vast age of the rainforests trumps all this in the strange sphere of my affections. Here on this island it is a key to the construction of time, and will likely become more so as the years roll by.

I wasn't always so conscious of the shaping presence of vast time. As a younger man I lamented the absence of the old in my island. I looked to Europe and its long heritage of unfolding culture. It was a perspective that was profoundly disrespectful of Aboriginal people's long immersion in the land, and it was misplaced in other ways, too. Then I discovered the ancient forests, and Europe seemed a mere playful pup by comparison. I knew that I lived in a country of vast age, that I had been welcomed within it, gathered up in a deep, knowing stream of time. I could feel its cool, wise breath upon me.

I look to the snippets of poetry with which I have seasoned my essay. They are dark. It is to the gothic in the forests that I have responded. This is real. To be lost in the rainforest, even if you know yourself not to be permanently lost, is to confront fear, to face mortality. Some of the quoted passages were written in reflection upon precisely those circumstances. But I would want, now, to be more celebratory, in keeping with the tone of this essay. I'll go away, give it a try.

On Skullbone Plains – Considering the False Contestation of Culture and Nature

(First published, under a different title, as a catalogue essay for the exhibition, *The Skullbone Experiment: A Paradigm of Art and Nature,* curated by Philip and Catherine Wolfhagen for the Tasmanian Land Conservancy, March-May 2014 Queen Victoria Museum, Launceston, July-September, UNSW Galleries, Sydney.)

Leaving Hobart. Bitumen, traffic lights, houses, commerce. A human place. Up the Derwent Valley, then turning north, climbing, leaving the bitumen, marginal pasture fading into the eternal bush, ragged abandoned fence-lines. Through cattlegrids and gates, the road rutted now, the ORV bucketing up through the bush. Onto Skullbone Plains. Not a human place. A natural place.

To the west is Lake Ina and, beyond the lake, the Cradle Mountain-Lake St Clair National Park. A scape of romance, that, all jagged crag and bejewelled, myrtle-fringed lake, an alpine tract irrelevantly memorialising the gods and sublime places of European antiquity. What impresses is the contrast. There is nothing romantic about Skullbone Plains. This place is, if a word is to capture it, *grim*. Scribbly knobs of tormented forest frame long runways of sub-alpine moor and fen sloping gently upwards from northeast to southwest and potted with shallow, unpretentious tarns buffered by snake-haunted bog. The place is as grim as its name. Nature, I am reminded, is not a synonym for beauty.

I am with scientists, and they know the natural systems that have shaped this upland plain. They tell me that, at the time of the last glaciation, a mere blip away in the vast chronicle of life on earth, the surface on which I would have stood was very many metres above my vantage today. The land here, indeed, is a creation of those times. I stand on a low barrier wall. It is unremarkable to the eye, a moraine left by the retreating ice – but what a barrier it is. The endangered *Clarence galaxias* thrives here, this unobtrusive moraine barring access to the voracious introduced brown trout.

On low knobs of rock snowgum thrives, a herd species huddling for comfort and sustenance. In the frost hollows eucalypts fail, keep a wary distance. Except for the marvellous cider gum. Here it stands in splendid isolation, its trunk an improbable twist of startling ribbons of colour, its sugary sap a wine-red bleed that richly complicates the trunk's sinuous, parti-coloured river. Across its range the cider gum is in decline, yet here it seems still to thrive. I camp on the fringe of a stand of young ciders – but this is a solitary entity, not a herd tree at all, and the young forest – most of it, perhaps all – will fall victim to marsupial grazing.

On these plains endangered species are given nurture, among them the charismatic spotted-tailed quoll. Unseen animals abound, the moorlands a carpet of scat. The skies are the realm of majestic avian predators, the wedgie, the white goshawk, the masked owl, even, counter-intuitively, the sea-eagle. Scientists have found 45 new animal species and collected 2,000 animal and plant species for classification and description. I learn much from Bruce, my namesake, an ex-Gunns forester, a man to whom I warm, would like to spend time with, a man from whom, I know, I could learn very much more.

When I go to wild places I look down to the complicated small worlds at my feet. Here is evolution's flamboyance. Here it is always showtime. Look about you on Skullbone Plains and there's that stern panorama of my initial impression. Look down and you encounter a world of wonder. In the sphagnum beds exquisite shapes and colours impose, demand engagement. Look deep within the herb fields and find there a riot of beauty that eludes the horizontal and expansive gaze. Look through the ponds and the runnels of water that thread the moss beds and the herb fields, and there you will see forms of grotesque fascination. Look into water. Always water. This is a world of water. It slides through the long ramps of glacial plain, holding the elements of the land in dynamic relation, informing all, the element that shapes and dominates all that is here. Look down to the life at your feet and you will know this.

The trending of my thought shifts. The scientists are here to support another cohort, an assemblage of many of Australia's finest visual artists, several Tasmanians among them. What will they make of this forbidding, unromantic land? Will they find the beauty within it that I have found by looking down to the small and the secret? Will they, with their developed artistic sensibilities, even need to look that far? Must they seek beauty at all? We gather beneath open canvas to eat and to talk, and not all our talk is of Skullbone Plains. Behind the eating area is a lurid scatter of tents. A helicopter is expected. This, it occurs to me, is a quintessentially cultural event, an event, moreover, designed to yield specifically cultural outcomes. There is a political point to our gathering. I look from the communal space down the long ramp of plain, and I begin to see it differently.

What I'm seeing is a road. An Aboriginal highway. It takes no great act of imagination to see a pelt-clad people working up the waterlogged plain towards us. One of them carries a firestick, applies it now, and a screen of smoke slips over the moor. I am witnessing an agricultural process, and it, too, is a shaping agent of the Skullbone Plains on which I walk today. It occurs to me that it is not far to the north, just a few ridges thence, that the remnant of the Big River people fell in with that master of humbug, George Augustus Robinson, choosing their own time and place to do so and thereby bringing the 'Black War' to an undemonstrative end. Artefactual traces of the people for whom Skullbone Plains was a seasonal home remain visible, I am told, to those who know where to look. The configuration of the very land could be described in these terms.

Now come trappers, snarers, and these people, too, lay a net of stories upon the land, and the print of their coming folds onto the fabric of the place. Cattle, too, and those who attend them. Old and weathered fenceposts, bearded with lichen. Tangles of rusted wire, entwined within tussock and shrub. Europeans, too, learn to know and love these unforgiving plains. Shelters are built. At the edge of a snowgum forest, overlooking the shallow expanse of Kenneth Lagoon, is a ruined hut. Tumbled stone fireplace. Rusted galvo. A four-gallon drum. Bedsprings. A battered, improvised frying pan. The story is told that one of the owners, in a blind rage, fired the hut to spite his partner, forgetting that it was his own beloved shanty, too. This may, of course, be an extremely un-urban urban myth. Then finally comes Gunns and the fraught dream of industrial logging. What *can* they have been thinking of? But that tenure passes, too – a mere ten percent logged and not much harm done.

All these waves of people. It is not, after all, a natural place.

In the communal camp the great Imants Tillers is reading Heidegger. He strikes a philosophic mood in me, too. In western thought, culture and nature are dichotomous – irreconcilable antonyms. And in the trend of western thought it is nature that gets the worst of it. There is no nature, runs the argument. All is culture. There is no part of the globe in which the impact of human activity is not present – and, thus, nature is dead. I sight down the long ramp of plain. Here is a land formed by inexorable glacial forces, forces that human agency could neither deflect nor stand against. The configuration of snowgum forest and treeless plain is similarly determined by grand climatic forces that proceed with blithe disregard for the clever species. And yet... yet... the plains are alive with the presence of humans. With culture.

I return to Hobart, sit on my deck, look out and over the southern suburbs. A ragtag riot of yellow-tailed black cockatoos cavorts, raucous and joyful, through the old elms in the quarter-acre blocks below. Little flashes of energy darting though the leaves of my backyard blackwood are silvereyes. The natural world is here, vibrant and vivid, in these inner suburbs. Can Hobart, then, be deemed a cultural place when it is so saturated with nature? If it is true that there is no such thing as nature because the imprint of human culture is ubiquitous, penetrating even to the deepest canyons of the oceans, then so must it be that there is no such thing as culture, because there is no part of the human realm into which the tenacious *presence* of natural forces cannot be found. 'Nature' and 'culture', I conclude, retain relevance as ideal-types, as fundamental principles at work in the world. They are processes, not fixed entities. Any defined space will be a mix of the two, and whether we deem it 'cultural' or 'natural' is a matter of the respective weight accorded the rival 'principles'.

All this portentous speculation from engagement with the charged landscape of a potent place, one not conventionally beautiful, yet extraordinary, emotionally overwhelming. I have no idea what the visual artists there with me will have taken from their own encounters with Skullbone Plains. But I know that it will be memorable.

On Albatross Island – Science and Myth

(Originally written as a catalogue essay for Matthew Newton and Richard Wastell's exhibition, *On Albatross Island*, curated by Emma Bett for the Bett Gallery, Hobart, 2015.)

The wind roars in from the west, scouring exposed conglomerate rock, funnelling into the cave where a party of humans seeks vain relief from the angry elements. Rachael Alderman is here. She is a government wildlife biologist and, since 2003, co-ordinator and team leader of a long-term monitoring study of the shy albatross. Photographer extraordinaire, Matt Newton, is here, and so is Richard Wastell, a beloved friend and an artist rapidly scaling his calling's heights. The shy albatross is here – though not *precisely* here. It is outside in the weather, fixed and resolute upon its flowerpot nest.

What is anomalous here is the presence of Newton and Wastell. This is aptly-named Albatross Island, 18 wild hectares 35kms out in the very teeth of the Bass Strait westerlies. To land on this island you need a permit – and if you are not a scientist your chances of securing one are virtually non-existent. Yet Newton and Wastell are here, for this is to be a collaborative science/art exercise in communication. More about that science/art nexus later. Why, though, should there be any call for such a project in the first place?

Rachael talks to me of the biology of the shy albatross. She outlines the nature of the monitoring program that has existed since 1980, and the history of human interaction with Albatross Island. It is an extraordinary story, one that features near-extinction – from 10-12000 breeding pairs when Bass and Flinders landed on the island in 1798, the shy albatross had declined to a mere 300-400 a century later. In the twentieth century the species recovered, climbing towards half its pre-contact population. Since 2005, though, the number of breeding pairs has again undergone a small but steady attrition.

The bird only breeds on three remote Tasmanian islands and, though Albatross Island is off limits to you and I, it is the most accessible of the three and it is here that the project is based. Rachael speaks of 'her' albatross with passion. It spends most of its life at sea, but Rachael knows it with a unique intimacy. After a day of banding and fitting miniature satellite tracking devices her hands and forearms stream blood. These are the wounds of love; they mark an engaged scientist's deep affection for an extraordinary bird, one hovering on the brink of vulnerability. She wants it lodged in the hearts and minds of Tasmanians. She wants it known and iconic. Which is where Newton and Wastell come in.

*

'Albatross Island.' I am struck by the mythical portent inherent in those conjoined words. There is a context for this project that sends it soaring into rarefied realms. Let's take 'island'.

As a geographic trope, the island 'idea' constructs much of civilised societies' self-understandings. The life humans live, or might live, is simultaneously distilled and made luminous on islands – islands real and islands imagined. The island is the crucible within which utopian dreams are played out. It concentrates a can-do sense and it concentrates the passions. Albatross Island is a remote speck in Bass Strait, but Bass and Flinders were here, Robinson was here with Trucanini and Wooraddy, the lawless sealers of the Strait were here. It is a place with a call on history. But its human history and its natural history have been profoundly incompatible. The sealers, having cleared the island of seals, then commenced plundering the albatross colonies to satisfy a pampered European taste for feathered pillows. A natural catastrophe was narrowly averted.

And here we have an all-too-familiar tale. Writing in 1987, that fine chronicler of the natural world, David Quammen, observed that in the preceding 300 years 127 species of bird had entered the dark cave of extinction – and of these 116 had lived on islands. Here's what he observed in his melancholic essay, 'Island Getaway':

> Speciation and extinction tend to happen more rapidly on islands. At the same time, the level of species diversity is almost always lower than on the continental mainlands. Therefore the complex relationships balancing life against death, stasis against change, the success of one species against the decline of another, show themselves more clearly in such places. The history of life on islands reflects – in a heightened and simplified way – the entire evolutionary process.

Evolution speeds up on islands, then. It throws up biological anomalies, flightlessness in birds, say, or gigantism. And that's fine, as long as the random evolutionary whims at play on any given island are left to unfold free from disturbance. But this rarely happens. At some point the cocooning isolation is breached, and then we see just how vulnerable are these little oceanic oases of uniquely evolved life. The isolation that made evolutionary *pizzazz* possible now becomes the problem – the island's hard edge becomes an imprisoning wall, precluding escape. And so the short march to extinction begins, most visibly as a consequence of human rapacity, but also subtly – with little genetic variation, susceptibility to introduced pathogens is heightened in island-dwelling species.

It has been said that islands are evolution's 'natural laboratories'. The role they have played in the emergence and subsequent development of evolutionary science is incalculable. The twin fathers of evolution, Darwin and Wallace, each formulated his breakthrough theory from observations made of life on islands

– indeed, Wallace published his pioneering study under the title, *Island Life*. In more recent times, MacArthur and Wilson's 1967 book, *The Theory of Island Biogeography,* set the agenda for a generation of ecological scientists. The Albatross Island scientific monitoring program, then, takes place within the very heartland – the island heartland – of evolutionary science. It stands four-square within a great tradition.

*

The shy albatross, though, is an ocean wanderer. It *should*, theoretically, be able to escape the prison of its breached island boundaries. Not so. Its dependence on a mere three of the planet's countless islands, from which it shows no inclination to diversify, gives the lie to this. Each admirably monogamous pair produces just a single egg each breeding season, and having hatched, these must survive the perils of sea and land for six years before they can begin to breed. Not easy in these fraught and crowded times. The trend of post-2005 decline suggests that the bird is succumbing to unprecedented and growing pressures within their land and, especially, marine environments.

This is not to be borne. Let's return to our portent-laden name: 'Albatross Island'. We have seen that the 'island' half of the name is loaded with scientific symbolism. What of 'albatross'?

It would be difficult to understate the place of the albatross as a defining motif within the cultural legacy of the English speaking world. This is because the killing of an albatross, along with the dire consequences of that act, is the theme of one of the greatest literary works in the English language, Samuel Taylor Coleridge's 'The Rime of the Ancient Mariner'.

In the maritime mythology of the English-speaking world the albatross was a harbinger of good fortune. So it was in Coleridge's poem:

> And a good south wind sprung up behind,
> The Albatross did follow,
> And every day, for food or play,
> Came to the mariners' hollo!

Given the several centuries during which Britannia ruled the waves, it may be that the strength of this superstition was crucial to the survival of albatross species in those wont-of-sympathy times. In any case, in Coleridge's poem the sailors' taboo is transgressed: 'with my cross-bow', the accursed Mariner tells the hapless Wedding Guest, 'I shot the Albatross'. As the poem unfolds, the doomed ship and its doomed crew descend into a tormented, parched and putrid hell:

> Water, water every where
> And all the boards did shrink;
> Water, water every where
> Nor any drop to drink.

In the poem, then, Coleridge, more than a century and a half ahead of his time, uses the killing of an albatross to embody a profound ecological imperative. The albatross is symbolic of the living spirit within all life, a spirit that we should hold sacrosanct. The animal world in particular merits our kindly regard and, indeed, our own wellbeing as a species is dependent upon the cultivation of just such a cast of mind. The Mariner's message is one for our own times, and it is the fate of the albatross that emblemises this. Nor is this just me being fanciful, for Coleridge makes his lesson explicit: 'He prayeth well', says the Mariner to the Wedding Guest, 'who loveth best/ Both man and bird and beast.'

Let's not mince words, then. Central to the canon of English literature is the albatross as the icon for ecological integrity. It is the single most prominent symbol of the need to prevent species destruction. No other creature has borne, into the present day, such dramatic import. This given, it is unconscionable, it seems to me, that we should passively watch the albatross slide into the dark cave of non-being with all those other lost, lamented species. With it would go our cultural soul. With it the battle must necessarily be deemed lost.

*

In the late 1950s, C.P. Snow, acclaimed scientist and celebrated novelist, made his famous distinction between the 'two cultures'. In western society, he observed, an intellectual schism divides the humanities and sciences, with each ignorant about the very basics of the other and, moreover, with little respect for the epistemologies from which each proceeds. Snow was harshest on the humanities, and a backlash within those realms eventually led him, in the 1960s, to produce a sunnier prognosis, one in which divisions were smoothing out into what he called a 'third culture'.

Perhaps. Many in the humanities are now literate in the new physics, ecology, nano and cyber technologies, and even new-wave neuroscience. The populisers of science can take much credit for this – books by, for example, Stephen Jay Gould, Paul Davies, Jared Diamond, the aforementioned David Quammen, and many others have been, and continue to be, runaway best sellers. Stephen Hawking and Richard Dawkins are household names. And on television popular science programs proliferate, turning their charismatic presenters into instant celebrities. For their part, scientifically-trained people are increasingly prominent within music, the visual arts and even literature. You may even encounter scientists at poetry festivals!

But it would be silly to take this too far. Mystification and wont of sympathy flourish on both sides, a situation not helped by dismissals, within the various post-modernisms that currently command the field in the humanities, of the 'essentialist' truth claims of science. The argument here is that science is just another hegemonic story seeking to disguise self-interest and context-dependent 'truth' under an entirely spurious claim to universality. Some scientists have hit back by attacking the validity of metaphor-sourced paths to truth and knowledge – a case fatally undermined by the fact that all major scientific advances found their initial eureka moments in metaphor, conceptually in some cases, or via a visual equivalent in others.

The bedrock credibility of science as an enterprise has been so undermined that when scientific findings seem to challenge sacred ideological precepts, as climate science has for the ideologues of the fundamentalist right of politics, it is easy enough to assert the validity of unquestioned ideological assumptions over the truth claims of science. However you cut it, science is in trouble, its declining fortunes reflected in ever-shrinking public budgets. It needs help, and help is most particularly needed at the point at which science butts against a largely non-scientific public. It has a communications crisis, and it needs to find new, more effective ways of getting its message 'out there'.

So. Albatross Island. One scientific story among very many, but a compelling one, a story, as we have seen, of immense symbolic import, touching chords (and cords) that extend deep into the very roots of evolutionary science, and into the mainstream of cultural iconography. Enter Newton and Wastell, artists drawn to the rough and rugged soul of a rough and rugged place – two of Tasmania's great visual interpreters, and at the height of their powers. They were up for it – and they were also up *to* it. Here is a collaboration born in heaven (as I might say if I believed in heaven). The visual arts communicate truths in a way that sits radically apart from the empirical rigours of the scientific method, but which entirely complements it. An image acts as a stiletto penetrating instantaneously to the bright heart of a truth. This is an ineffable insight, its impact working slowly through the viewer's constructed reality long after the initial exposure, quietly reconfiguring sympathies and core understandings. The communicative effect of a skilfully wrought visual image may be immeasurable, but it is of great potential power.

Albatross Island is an extraordinary place, the shy albatross an extraordinary creature, Rachael Alderman and her team of extraordinarily dedicated scientists at work on an extraordinary project. They deserve the talents of these extraordinary visual artists. Here is a collaboration that should ink the shy albatross upon that signature list that sums up an island's soul, placing this marvellous bird at the centre of Tasmanians' constructed sense of their vibrant home.

Resurrecting the Public Interest – On Logging Lapoinya

(First published as 'Home Is Where Our Heart Is', a 'Talking Point' article in *The Mercury*, 18 March, 2016. The residents of Lapoinya, it will be remembered, lost their battle.)

Early in 2016 the small North-West hamlet of Lapoinya tried unsuccessfully to prevent the government-sanctioned logging of a much-loved tract of eucalypt forest on their very doorstep. The community's anguish was palpable, strong. Government, though, was immovable, locked, as it was, into a recognizable and long-standing discourse in which opposition to forest operations could only be constructed around questions of 'old growth' and 'threatened species'. Neither applied to Lapoinya – so that, as far as the authorities were concerned, was that.

And they were wrong. Let's step back into first principles.

When a government, or a government instrumentality, makes a 'big call', a policy decision likely to prove controversial, the bottom-line defence of its position is that it is in 'the public interest'.

Rightly so. There can be no democratic politics without a concept of 'the public interest'. It is the bedrock from which democracy proceeds. Without a claim to be acting 'in the public interest' a government has no mandate for making decision *a* rather than decision *b*. This is what confers *legitimacy* upon any and all acts of government and public instrumentalities. Policy decisions that are in the public interest are legitimate; those that are *not* in the public interest are not legitimate. Even the extreme individualism of neo-liberalism, the values paradigm within which both major parties function, must have recourse to a concept of 'the public interest' – as already noted, without it no government or public body can claim legitimate authority for its actions.

There are, though, public interest claims that trump those of government. There are publics within publics. The public interest claims of government are generalised and diffuse. Within any political system there will also be intermediate public interests, and strong interests quite specific to smaller, more coherent publics. The smaller and more homogeneous are these publics – neighbourhoods in which there is a broad commonality of place values, for example – the more likely it is that this less diffuse public interest can, with confidence, be identified. There are cogent reasons why the interests of these publics should be accorded precedence over larger, more diffuse publics.

The interests of all publics within the public sphere are legitimate, but those of localised publics are systematically under-acknowledged by public authorities. This is understandable because such authorities, as agencies of the state, are inclined to assume that there is only one public interest – *the* public interest – that of the entire state.

But there is a persuasive case that the interests of local and regional publics constructed around a shared sense of place should be given precedence over other interests – not only the private interests of individuals, but also the state's interest in promoting economic activity. As we move from local articulations of a public interest to those that apply to a larger, more complex 'public' – an entire political system, for example, or, in the case of a system such as ours, a sub-system as complex as a state within a larger federation – the 'public' interest becomes 'smeared out' and much more difficult, beyond the broadest of parameters, to determine. A public interest locally articulated should take precedence because its concentrated character makes for a stronger, more coherent public claim.

Strongly articulated local public interest claims will almost always cohere around a passionate commitment to place. Violation of an affectionately regarded place induces distress, even grief, in those who are forced to witness the defilement of that place. Planning regimes and government agencies are blind to this and, sadly, tragedies systematically ensue.

Deeply felt place attachment is, then, the big sleeper within government and agency policy determinations. It is mostly ignored — and this is why determinations made in Hobart that have consequences in, let us say, little Lapoinya (back there in the bush behind my home town 'up the Coast'), typically generate so much political heat. Yet it is increasingly recognised that the construction of place identity and attachment is a fundamental human activity, and the need to 'belong' within a shared geography is the equivalent of such basic human needs as liberty, sustenance, and security from violence. 'A deep relationship with place', the geographer Edward Relph asserted back in the 1970s, is 'as necessary, and perhaps as unavoidable, as close relationships with people. Without such relationships human existence is bereft of much of its significance'.

This means that any activity that harms or 'makes over' a valued place, threatening the depth of a community's relationship with it by degrading the qualities of that place, is against the public interest. Where a community can demonstrate a deep sense of a shared commitment to place, to a communally-defined 'home', that attachment merits a respectful regard. When it is not respected — when it is over-ridden by the actions of a government or public authority — an unwarranted, grief-inducing violation of an insufficiently acknowledged but basic human need has taken place.

This, then — the strong and tangible public interest of local and regional communities in the maintenance of the valued qualities associated with a treasured place – establishes a prior public interest, one that can be shown to be superior to the use-rights of individuals and to the 'promoting economic activity' interests of governments, and it entitles local communities to have the prime say in determining the future and the evolving character of 'their' place.

Which explains what has happened in Lapoinya, and why the interests of the local community should have prevailed. It matters not that the forest scheduled for logging is not 'old-growth'. It matters that a government agency, with the government's connivance, chose, we now know, to *lose* money in a logging operation undertaken, we have to conclude, with the aim of disturbing the peace in order to showcase a draconian, brand-spanking-new, anti-protest law. And all this in violation of a public's interest that should be accorded precedence – because the forest in contention is central to the Lapoinya people's strongly articulated place meaning. And that should simply be that.

Until governments acknowledge the prior rights that deep communal place attachment confers, we can expect more of these locally distressing confrontations. To build the priority of place into planning and policy systems will be devilishly difficult, and it will be a significant constraint upon economic development and government activity. It is just that the concentrated interest of local publics in preserving the integrity of deeply loved local place trumps the public interest claims of governments, and it is time that this was recognised.

Schismatic Tasmania and the Politics of Writing

(This is a slightly amended version of 'Tasmanian Writing and the Great Tasmanian Dichotomy', published in February 2018 in *Island* 152, and itself a very much revised version of 'Memory in a Fractured Island: An Introduction to the Literature of the Island at the End of the Earth', presented at *The Tower at the End of the World, a Conference on Islands and Literature* at Tórshavn, Faroe Islands, 11 May 2017.)

When transportation of British convicts to Van Diemen's Land ended in 1853, a fierce backlash set in, a backlash against remembrance, and against history itself. In symbolic burial of what was deemed a shameful past the island was renamed Tasmania, and the convict past was ignored – even denied. So, too, was the destruction of Aboriginal society and the attempted annihilation of the first people here.

By 1880 it was possible to write boosterist accounts of Tasmania with minimal reference to its still-recent convict past – and the first post-convict generation pursued a priggish respectability with the sort of determination a subject people might evince in pursuit of liberation. It achieved a narrow-minded gentility that perseveres today. The 1860s to 1890s thus saw the appalling unremarked tragedy of aging ex-convict couples shunned, ostracised by the families they had nurtured, their very existence hidden by their children from their grandchildren. Denied access to social approbation, the key to attaining respectability was to erase all traces connecting one to the past. 'Let the dead', it was often said, 'bury the dead', and elaborate fake genealogies were constructed to this end.

As for the people who were here when Europeans arrived, by now deemed to have been eradicated, the occasional reference to their putative disappearance was made neutrally, with only the occasional vague hint of regret, and certainly no acceptance of culpability on the part of the colonial invaders.

What this amounts to is an expunging of memory. A supreme example came to hand in 1996 when a young man with the face of an angel drove to the site of the key penal station, Port Arthur, by now a major tourist attraction, and went on a shooting spree, massacring 31 people in what was, at the time, the largest single-gunman massacre in peacetime history. In the outpouring of communal grief that ensued, the dominant note struck was one of loss of innocence, perpetrated, moreover 'at such an idyllic spot'. That the central institution of a system as brutal as convictism could ever be described as 'innocent' and 'idyllic' beggars belief. It emblemises the strength of the island's communal forgetting, a forgetting that was already in full swing in the later years of the nineteenth century, when there was a powerful sentiment in favour of obliterating the derelict complex of buildings at Port Arthur. The task of forgetting is much easier when there are no tangible reminders of what you would prefer to forget.

The focus of this comprehensive act of denial was, of course, the convict past, but it suited, too, the flaccid collective morality that also enabled European Tasmania to avoid engaging with the enormity of the obliteration and near genocide of a stable and functional resident Aboriginal society, and, in the first decades of the twentieth century, the deliberate extermination of the world's largest marsupial carnivore, the thylacine.

The challenge posed by our need to engage constructively with a dire recent past was our first test as an island people – and we failed it then, as we have been failing it since.

*

None of this is particularly original. The point I'd make, though, is this: as familiar as this case is to most Tasmanians who read and think inquiringly, there are many social groups for whom this would be an astounding revelation, one so apparently bizarre that it could not be deemed credible. To such people history is an arcane intellectual pursuit, the province of a bounded circle of people with a strange and unworldly obsession – because the world is what is unfolding around us on a daily basis, and the only thing that matters is the future.

All this notwithstanding, it is almost impossible to comprehend how such a full-blown exercise in memory obliteration could possibly be achieved. It is only attainable if the social focus is firmly fixed on the future, this being seen to be full of material promise, while to its achievement the past is deemed irrelevant. Thus, from early in the twentieth century the dominant Tasmanian dreaming had, as its centrepiece, the roar and throb of heavy industry, of clamour and dense, smoke-particled air. And the equally murky past could be ignored.

For such an hegemonic dreaming two perceptual conditions needed to be in place. One is the aforementioned determined rejection of memory. The second is a view of the island's material fabric that denies intrinsic worth to its living components, and to the complexity of processes that bind that livingness together. There is minimal understanding, beyond certain professional and enthusiastic but amateur cohorts, of the details of the island's flora and fauna and the conservation status of particular species. Almost no-one in the Tasmanian Parliament holds this knowledge, for instance. The health of the island's varied ecologies runs a distant second in official priorities to the ephemeral health of economic conditions. This given, the living fabric of the island can be treated as nothing more than a storehouse of resources to fuel the aspirant industrial economy, and containing no meaning or value beyond its reduction to the raw material needed to realise the dreams of industrial 'progress'.

This bipartisan industrial aspiration was eventually incompletely realised, and when the irresistible tides of globalisation arrived on the island, most Tasmanians were unprepared. The island's dreaming was shown to be misconceived – most spectacularly in the 2010 closure of the enterprise that emphatically embodied the industrial dreaming, the Burnie pulp mill – and this has compromised the strength of the narrative's hold on the hearts and minds of Tasmanians, though only slightly, and large numbers of Tasmanians adhere to it still.

Of the two axes of ignorance needed for the construction and maintenance of Tasmania's grand industrial dreaming, memory and ecology, it is the latter that has been most effectively challenged within the civic and political realms, primarily through the tumultuous impact of environmental protest movements, and the electoral successes of the Greens. Even so, the reaction to the coming of the Greens has largely been one of uncomprehending bewilderment shading into blind anger, the aspirational values base that the Greens represent being spectacularly misunderstood. The Greens *are* understood to stand for a valuing of life and living process over the narrowly economic, though *why* they should hold to such a values base is, for most people, thoroughly mystifying.

'For most people…' Yes, because here we have the most fundamental faultline within Tasmanian society. This is not capital vs labour. It is old ways of seeing versus new. The island has descended into two rival dreamings. The dominant one is adhered to by the mainstream of politics, business, bureaucracy, and the displaced industrial labour that is the principle victim of the wrecking ball of globalisation. The oppositional dreaming insists on the relevance of memory, on the need to look a dire history square in the face and not flinch from its moral consequences. And it insists on the primacy of ecological relationships over the narrowly economic. Those belonging to this oppositional dreaming are smaller in number, roughly comprising the 10-20 percent who vote Green, but including, too, a substantial number of people who adhere to old voting behaviours out of loyalty to what I would argue is misplaced partisan identity. A smaller cohort, then – but dominant within the island's intellectual and creative elites.

*

It is against this backdrop that Tasmanian writers write. Tasmania's writers are the prime insisters on the inevitability of memory; they are the constructors and deconstructors of island meanings old and new.

Foremost in this regard is Richard Flanagan, winner of the 2015 Man Booker award for *The Narrow Road to the Deep North*. His Booker prize winning novel is set mostly in occupied Thailand during World War II, and though this, too, is a Tasmanian story, more germane to my purpose is Flanagan's first novel, *Death of a River Guide*. This is the great book of the Tasmanian soul, a brash and passionate assertion of the extraordinary Tasmanian story – indeed, a project for its recovery, in all its intricate particulars. It is also a sorrowful and sorrowing book – it looks the darkness in the Tasmanian soul full in the face, and it does so with a great love for the land itself, and with a great human tenderness. The river guide in question is a young man of mixed ethnicity who shepherds parties of rafting tourists down the wild, rushing cauldron of the famed wilderness river, the Franklin. Struggling to make sense of his own sorry life, the guide is trapped in the river and is drowning. What he sees is not only a replay of his own life, but the life of the island. The stories the drowning river guide dreams are the stories Tasmanians grew up with, heard almost furtively in this place of no-memory, stories taken to be of no account in the larger scheme of things, those exciting worlds being far away on the other side of the planet. In our remote exile, we poor descendants of bog Irish peasants and the runts of the London slums, lived, we thought, lives of utter irrelevance.

When he published *Death of a River Guide* in 1994, to critical silence but to an avid, word-of-mouth generated readership, Flanagan told us, as he told the rest of Australia, that the island at the end of the Earth is a repository of extraordinary stories, of doings dark and wondrous, of passion and marvellous folly and heroic enterprise. Our stories, he said, are not boring, and though they may be sources of shame and humiliation, they should not be gathered up in an opaque communal amnesia. Flanagan turned a key and liberated a collective soul. Warts and all. In its wake a cultural confidence burgeoned. In all the arts there was a flowering, and central to this flowering was a loving but forensic engagement with Tasmania's ambiguous history and with its conflicted present. While the men of power, the repositories of the old dreaming, went on with their important business unperturbed, Tasmania's cultural practitioners, with writers in the van, went about the place-saving task of recovering memory.

In the huge shadow cast by Flanagan, writing flourished, and poetry in particular. I have called Tasmania 'an island of poets' so often that it has become a cliché. The island's poets so intensively engage with the natural world and are so determinedly set on recovering and interrogating its history, that Australian cultural discourse, looking in upon Tasmania, is frankly puzzled. This is not what contemporary Australian literature, determinedly urban and internationalist, is supposed to be about. I don't care. It is our journey – our process of discovery. And when you throw in poetic engagement with such island tropes as remoteness, the pervasiveness of the sea and the edge, the distilled experience that comes from living within bounds, all infused by an awareness that the island's bounds frame a startling and unique past, you get an equally unique poetics.

Not all our poets are aware of their participation in this project, and a small few simply aren't. Most, though, can articulate such a memory-recovering project – they write *of* Tasmania, *for* Tasmanians, and trawl the past to bring it into the present.

But this is a project to which the men of power are blithely oblivious. I wish I could plot a strategy for change, but I can't. The literary community is another of those Tasmanian silos, its practitioners largely writing for a minority of enthusiasts. I'd give plenty to know how to change this.

Books Are the New Zucchini

(First published June 2019, in *Island* 157.)

It's a familiar joke. Your backyard zucchini crop has ripened nicely. Trouble is, there are far more of the succulent green things than you can possibly use yourself. No matter – there are all those friends and relatives soon to be grateful for your largesse. But no – you are politely told to keep your zucchinis to yourself. (Well, okay, we'll take two.) Despair sets in. You've raised your zucchinis with tender loving care. You can't stand the thought of them going to compost. Besides, your depression grandparents brought you up to value food in all its manifestations. To waste is a sin against ecological and social justice. Guerrilla tactics are mandated. At two in the morning you again do the rounds of the domiciles of all your friends. You offload your zucchinis on their front doorsteps. You ring the doorbell. And then you run away.

Musicians have a variation on this joke. Tired of his beloved but deeply unfashionable banjo, a musician decides it is time to sell. He advertises its sale in the appropriate trade papers at a very reasonable price, but receives not a skerrick of interest. Desperate now, he does the rounds of the banjo-playing community, hoping to find a kindred soul who, perhaps recalling the sweet notes this old banjo has been known to produce, will take it off his hands. For a mere pittance. For nothing at all. And is met with amused and tolerant smiles. But our musician is a canny one. He takes himself off to a folk festival, parks his car prominently, and leaves it unlocked with the banjo on the back seat, confident that he will return at the end of the weekend to find his banjo gone. But no. He returns to find his car crammed to the absolute gun'ls – with old banjos.

This essay argues that books have become the new zucchini, the new banjo.

*

The chattersphere has never been so obsessed with books – with their status as physical and cultural property, with their future, with their peculiar attraction to so many people. Such an obsession was there throughout the twentieth century of course, but it seems to have increased in intensity in these technologically exuberant times. Our love of books has significantly ramped up; taken fire.

Much of the writing that this has generated has to do with the book's future; with its capacity to withstand technological ambush and unpredictable pummelling in the market. The consensus seems to be that the book has seen off the Kindle threat, and that we can put behind us the gloomy prognostications of a few years back. Whether the book can survive less specific threats posed by the turbulent global market seems less certain – and the predominant themes of writings upon writing mirror this. In front of me, for example, is a piece by Louise Adler, then CEO of Melbourne University Press, from *The Garret* in August 2018. Her focus is entirely upon the problematic axis between publisher, writer and market – and this is pretty typical. My focus is not. It's upon what happens to the book *after* it has run the gauntlet of genesis and birth, has lived its venerable life, and now seems to no longer contain any further use value. I've been moved to reflect upon this because no-one else seems to do so. In the curious literature of books, as with Adler's piece in *The Garret*, it's all about new books.

*

Anyone reading this essay will know the name, Marie Kondo, the Japanese guru of the de-cluttering movement. In her runaway best-seller, *The Life-Changing Magic of Tidying Up*, Kondo makes a case for the divestment of personal property. This is to be done by considering, on a category-by category basis, which individual items continue to give joy. All else is 'junk' and to be sloughed off. It is a seductive idea. In closing a program on de-cluttering, Paul Barclay, the host of *Big Ideas* on ABC Radio National told his audience: 'I don't know about you, but I'm off home to start de-cluttering – and I'm not even a hoarder'.

I can see it now – Paul, being as good as his word, heads straight for… his library. Because prominent – nay, pre-eminent – among the classes of 'junk' that the de-clutterists nominate, is, of course, 'books' (though presumably *The Life-Changing Magic of Tidying Up* is exempt from this). This is important. By 'clutter' one can almost read 'books'. Enter any house that could be deemed ripe for sustained de-cluttering, and in almost all instances, the dominant object within the 'clutter' is the book.

*

Allied to the decluttering movement, though conceptually distinct from it, is the trend in our times – a robust trend – to decorative minimalism. Largely driven from within architecture, where a desire to leave clean lines unadorned has become pre-eminent, this is reinforced by a wish for internal planes (let's call them walls) to remain void – blank, white, unexpressive of the personality of the people to be found within those walls. I'm tempted to write something I often say. Well, I will. Show me a house devoid of lovingly personalised artefacts, of mind-stimulating decoration, and I'll show you a person with a mind in which nothing much is happening.

Especially does this apply to books. The real tragedy of the de-clutterist's and decorative minimalist's approach to books is that it is blind to what books signify – that books ('books', as distinct from 'a book') speak of who we are. To those we invite into our space, and also to ourselves. It is a joy, and an instructive joy, to browse one's shelves, reminding oneself of encounters with other lives and insights, and reflecting on what those encounters have given us, how they have made us. Books constitute beloved objects, signposts along the paths that have taken us from our past to our present. Antidotes to existential angst, sustenance against the terrors of our times, against the demeaning loss of physicality as old age begins its inexorable approach.

Okay – I admit that I've been a tad harsh. My reference to looming old age reminds me that for very many people minimalism – in the form of downsizing – is not a choice. Your beautiful Edwardian house, with its delightfully adorned walls, its wonderfully complex garden, and its beloved library is too much. The kids have grown and fled. Your limbs creak and groan and you'll never climb a ladder again. You sell up and move to a smaller house, to a unit, into care. You *have* to divest – it is not a choice. And in this divestment, books, especially, have to go.

*

What are the options? The second-hand bookshop down the road will take selected items, but that hardly scratches the surface of the problem. You can do what the aging academics do in my university school – add unwanted books to a pile in the middle of the common room, a stratagem much favoured by those who face retirement and the clearing out of their office. Every time I look at that pile it gets bigger and hideously bigger. A friend of mine has a variation on this – she simply leaves unwanted books on the footpath outside her front gate, and she assures me this works. The tip shop and the op shops are good bets – you can clear a good many books that way, especially if your library contains a sizable portion of low-browish items. One interesting and creative ploy is to repurpose books as works of art, and if the artist is sufficiently ambitious, you can shift quite a few this way, too, though, of course, they will then have ceased to be works of learning or literature – as books, they are effectively dead. And then there's the fad of the pop-up library (admirable, though I'm about to give voice to a misgiving). They are everywhere, and they seem to work.

Or you can burn your books. When I grew up only Hitler thought it okay to burn books, and I came to believe that here was a sin akin to matricide. How quaint is such a view in the times in which we currently live!

*

A man from Quebec, in the Letters pages of *The Guardian Weekly* on August 31, 2018, writes of 'seeing huge recycling bins full of unwanted books at libraries and charity shops', and though it makes his 'heart beat faster when I hear of the "pure pleasure" that can still be derived from these discarded but still tactile, readable treasures', to me this is deeply ill-omened. It speaks of a time, the first since the invention of the book, when the (total) supply of books outweighs (total) demand.

The pop-up *library*. I can't help but think that such a device is itself symbolic of a deep malaise in the way we now look at books. The problem is to be found in that word 'library'. You can divest yourself of individual items, or even quite substantial chunks of your personal library, via one or more of those ploys noted above. But an entire library? And if yours is a learned library, you're completely sunk. A retired academic recently told me of the plight of Australia's most prestigious sociologist who, on *his* retirement (which time was a while ago now, and that's where my clues to his identity stop), was unable to find an academic library, an academic bookseller (these have pretty much vanished now, anyway), or a commercial bookseller willing to take the library off his hands. The point that I would make, though, is why should a library – any library – be sold as other than a collection entire of itself? Libraries should be passed complete (or at least as complete sub-sections) to young bibliophiles, should such people still exist. They will then add their own shaping signatures to those evolving libraries as the years roll by.

Pie in the sky. Both the decluttering movements and the decorative minimalism ethic are deeply antithetical to the notion of a personal library. For the decorative minimalist books are simply anathema to the desired aesthetic effect. To the anti-clutterist books have to be kept or discarded on an individual basis. I derive joy from this item – it stays, but everything else on the shelf goes. At the end of August, 2018, a week after the *World Health Organisation* officially classified hoarding as a medical disorder, *The Guardian* quoted an Edinburgh hoarder – a *book hoarder* – observing thus: '"If I was living in a big, posh house and had this amount of books on the shelves, they would call it a library", he said. "Nobody would go, 'Oh, Lord Toffington is a hoarder!' But because I'm living in a bungalow and I'm the underclass, I'm a hoarder."' With reluctance I'll set the pertinent class factor aside, and say I couldn't agree more – with the observation that, as housing becomes progressively smaller, it becomes much harder to set aside the requisite space for a library. This notwithstanding, to derive joy from *a collection* of books simply seems to be precluded by the procedures mandated by *The Life-Changing Magic of Tidying Up.*

The personal library, whichever way you cut it, seems doomed, then. Over the street from me live two writers, having moved there from a much larger house (yes, they downsized!). In their first house one writer installed, as fixtures, some beautiful floor to ceiling bookcases. He thought them one of the house's major selling points. Imagine his consternation when the estate agent, on entering the room, looked with dismay at the bookcases and said, 'oh, these will have to go!' Yes, the dice seem well and truly loaded against the survival of the personal library.

*

My knickers are in a twist well and truly, are they not? It's because I think the survival of books as beloved collections matters. Earlier, in connection with another point, I spoke of this in overly lyrical prose. More of this now.

There's a much better book doing the rounds than *The Life-Changing Magic of Tidying Up*, though it is attracting far less attention (well that's the way of things these days). It's Alberto Manguel's *Packing My Library*, and everyone who has been seduced by Marie Kondo's case for getting rid of books should read Manguel's thoroughly convincing corrective. Most significantly, Manguel's focus is not on the enchantment of the individual book, but on the enchantment of books in the collective – on the *library*.

For Manguel the library is not only tactile and tangible – it approximates a living thing. His library has a physicality that ebooks or even individual 'real' items could never have. He wants its 'solid presence'; he wants shapes, textures. He refers to his books as 'very much like breathing creatures', and 'after the library was packed and the movers came... I would hear the books calling out to me in their sleep'.

Not all of us would want to go so far, but a library certainly has a significance in one's life that is hard to under-estimate. Manguel says it perfectly: 'I've often felt that my library explained who I was, gave me a shifting self that transformed itself constantly through the years'. He looks at his library and reads his autobiography. He also finds, therein, 'the possibility of enlightening conversation... the memory of friendships that required no introduction'.

All this is beyond the ken of the de-clutterists, for whom a book is a book, and for whom the transcendent meaning of a library — books in collectivity — simply does not register. To idle along the shelves, fingers running reflectively along spines, slowly putting together the components of your personal evolution, thoughts and memories sifting gently through a quiet day's soft light — this is the glory of the personal library. Not the individual book, but this book, that book and all these other books in wondrous synergy.

And yet, the personal library appears to be doomed. I have conceded that for economic and other reasons the accumulation of a personal library is often not an option, but it has hitherto been *de riguer* for those living a learned or creative life. Divestment of his library is actually not a problem for Manguel, because his grief was only brought on by the need to dismantle and pack his library as he prepared to shift continents. For others the situation is more dire. Caught, now, in the pincers of the decluttering fad and the trend to decorative minimalism I regard my beloved library and wonder how I'll dispose of it when my day comes. If you hear a scuffling sound on your front step in the wee hours, followed by a discreet knock, you know what you'll find when you open the door, don't you. A hint: it won't be zucchini.

www.ingramcontent.com/pod-product-compliance
Lightning Source LLC
Chambersburg PA
CBHW020255030426
42336CB00010B/780